Physics 1AA3:
Introduction to Modern Physics

Laboratory Manual

Last updated: January 2018

Edited by: Tara Power

Please send any comment you have about this manual (errors, typos, ...) to:

powert@mcmaster.ca
fradin@physics.mcmaster.ca
nejat@physics.mcmaster.ca

Introduction

Table of Contents

PART I: INTRODUCTION

1. WHY DO PHYSICS LABS? 3
2. ASKING GOOD QUESTIONS 4
3. DESIGNING AND PERFORMING GOOD EXPERIMENTS 5
4. KEEPING GOOD NOTES 6
5. EVALUATING DATA USING EXCEL 6
6. ERROR ANALYSIS 8
7. THE CORRECT USE OF SIGNIFICANT DIGITS 13
8. COMMON UNCERTAINTY AND SIGNIFICANT DIGIT PROBLEMS 14
9. PRE-LABS 16
10. LAB REPORT BREAKDOWN 17
11. HOW TO ANALYZE DATA 18
12. SAMPLE COVER SHEET 26
13. LAB REPORT MARKING SCHEME 27
14. FEEDBACK FORM 27

Part II: EXPERIEMENTS

1. LAB #1: THE VITRUVIAN MAN 29
2. LAB #2: ROTATIONAL MOTION 34
3. LAB #3: THE ELECTROCARDIOGRAM 43
4. LAB #4: MAGNETOTACTIC BACTERIA 52

Part I: Introduction

1. Why do Physics labs?

You may be wondering why we are asking you to complete Physics laboratory experiments, especially since these labs take time and care to complete, and might seem challenging to you, when you might not be considering a career having to do with Physics.

The first reason for completing Physics laboratory experiments is that it will help you better assimilate the material you are learning in class. Whether you complete a lab after or before the corresponding material is covered in class, actively participating in a related experiment will help you understand and memorize this material, especially those of you who are tactile learners.

The second, and maybe most important reason for completing Physics labs is that they teach you about the *scientific method*. All of you in this course are working towards a degree in Science, and our scientific knowledge is built upon the design and interpretation of astute and reliable experiments. During these Physics labs, you will be taught to formulate a hypothesis, to design and conduct your own experiment in collaboration with your lab partners, to analyze your data in a scientific manner using computer software, to compare your results with the predictions of theory or with the results of other experiments and to evaluate their significance, and to write a scientific report. Further, you will learn to do this in a safe and ethical way. All these skills are important for scientists, and you should be able to transfer them to other science courses, and to use them during your future career as a scientist.

Note that the labs are mandatory. You cannot pass this course unless you have completed ALL the laboratory experiments listed in this manual and submitted a lab report for each of them. Talk to your instructor or TA as soon as possible to arrange for a make-up if you miss one of the labs.

Introduction

2. Asking good questions

In most of the labs described in this manual, each lab group will have to start by asking its own question. This question should of course be related to the topic of the lab. We suggest that you come to the lab with already an idea for one or several questions, which you can then discuss with your lab partners and with a TA, before definitely settling on a single question per group.

Your question should be formulated as a hypothesis. Basically, it means that you will need to take sides and say what you think the answer to your question will be. For example, instead of asking "How does the frequency of a pendulum vary with the initial velocity of the pendulum?", a scientist will prefer to say "My hypothesis is that the frequency of a pendulum is independent of the initial velocity of the pendulum".

A good hypothesis is falsifiable, meaning that it is possible to prove or disprove it (compare: "The frequency of a pendulum is independent from its initial velocity" and "God exists"). In your case, a good hypothesis is one that you can prove or disprove using the equipment at your disposal in the lab and during the time allotted.

A good question should be asked in relation to a context, in other word there should be a motivation for asking the question. For example, if you are presented with a theory, a natural question to ask is whether this theory, or a specific aspect of this theory is correct. The more familiar you are with the topic of the lab, the easier it will be to ask pertinent questions. So we recommend you read the background information given to you for each of the experiments described in this manual, and also go back to the corresponding material covered in class, <u>before</u> you go into the lab.

The best hypotheses are quantitative, meaning that you are not just looking for trends in your observations, but you are looking for a quantitative agreement between your data and a particular theory. For example, compare: "The frequency of a pendulum increases with the length of the pendulum" and "The period of a pendulum, T, increases with the length of a pendulum, L, so that $T = \sqrt{L}$ ". Both hypotheses are correct, but the second is much more interesting, because it can be a test of Newton's second law, and can lead to a measurement of the gravitational constant g.

Finally, a great question is interesting, meaning that you should be able to get an audience excited about what the answer will be, meaning that <u>you</u> should be interested about what the answer will be. So rather than trying to be conservative when asking your question, try to be curious and inventive.

Introduction

3. Designing and performing good experiments

In order to obtain precise and reliable results, you need to think carefully about your experimental design. Think about the following points.

- What are you going to measure? Remember that you are doing this experiment to answer a question. So what can you measure to make sure that this question will be answered? If your hypothesis is "The frequency of a pendulum is independent from its initial velocity", then obviously you want to measure the frequency of the pendulum for different initial velocities, but which range of initial velocities are you going to use (the larger the range, the easier to see whether there is a dependence on velocity)? How are you going to measure the initial velocity? How can you make sure that no other variable is changed when varying the velocity?

- How are you going to measure? Make sure you think about the best way to make your measurements, in order to reduce experimental errors to a minimum (for example, in the case of the pendulum, you might want to measure 10 periods and then divide the result by 10, rather than measuring just 1 period, in order to reduce uncertainties related to determining the beginning and the end of a period).

- How many times are you going to repeat each measurement? A great way to estimate experimental errors is to repeat each measurement several times, in order to see how reproducible this measurement is. And if there are several persons in your group, it might be a good idea to repeat the experiment while changing the roles (for one set of experiments Paul is starting the pendulum and Josie is measuring the frequency, and for the next set of experiments, they exchange role), to make sure that you get an idea of what might be the influence of the experimentalist on the experiment.

- Should you perform control experiments? In some cases, it is very useful to have a control experiment (for example, if your hypothesis is "For a blue pendulum, frequency is independent of initial velocity", then don't forget to check what happens for a red pendulum).

When you write your report, it should be apparent that you thought about these questions before performing your experiment.

Introduction

4. Keeping good notes

Good note keeping is another important quality for a scientist. Try to be thorough and precise when keeping notes of what you are doing. Instead of just writing numbers when measuring something, don't forget to write the date, who performed the measurement, what were the conditions of this experiment, the units of the measurement, etc... And make sure you can reread your own notes. Feel free to write notes in handwritten format, or in electronic format if you prefer and if you are able to bring your own laptop.

5. Evaluating data using Excel

The use of computer software to analyze experimental data allows for consistency, reliability and speed. There are many different commercially available products that can be used for data analysis. In this class we will mainly use Microsoft Excel, because of its widespread and easy use.

We will introduce you to different functions of Excel as we go through the different laboratory experiments, but if you have no prior experience with Excel, it might be a good idea to get familiar with this software in advance. There are many free tutorials available online, for example:

http://homepage.cs.uri.edu/tutorials/csc101/pc/excel97/excel.html

5.1 PLOTTING YOUR DATA

1. Name the columns you want to plot (enter the name just above the data)
2. Select the columns you want to plot.
3. Do: Insert -> Chart -> XY(scatter) -> Anything. Click "Next".
4. Select "Source data", then remove the series you don't want to plot, and name the series you do want to plot. Click "Next".
5. Customize your graph by adding axis labels, legends, changing the axis scale, etc...
6. When you are done press "Finish".
7. Double-clicking on the data sets should give you the option to add error bars to your data. Chose the option "Custom" and then select the range of cells where your errors are entered both of the "+" and "-"errors.

Introduction

5.2 ANALYZING YOUR DATA

To check whether there is a linear correlation between lengths 1 and 2:

1. Select the data on the chart, by clicking on any data point.
2. Do: Chart -> Add trend line.
3. Select: Type -> Linear. A linear fit of your data should appear on the chart.
4. Select: Options -> Display equation & display R-squared. An equation should appear on the chart.
5. If you are looking for a proportional relationship between your two variables, you can set the intercept to 0 by selecting: Options -> Set intercept = 0.

5.3 SAVING YOUR DATA

1. Save your completed Excel file, by doing: File -> Save As -> ...
2. To save your chart for inclusion in a text editor, select your chart and do: File -> Save As -> Format: pdf, tif or jpg -> ...

6. Error analysis

A quantity measured as the result of an experiment is meaningless unless we have an idea of the error associated with that quantity. Imagine for example that you are a forensic scientist in charge of investigating the untimely death of Colonel Mustard, found dead in the Thode library this morning. Your best estimate is that he was murdered at 9:45pm last night. Does this mean that Miss Scarlett is innocent, since it is known for a fact that last evening she was the Phoenix until exactly 10pm? It all depends on the uncertainty associated with your measurement. If you are confident your estimate is correct give or take 5 mins, then Miss Scarlett is innocent. If, on the other hand, your estimate is only correct give or take 30 mins, then Miss Scarlett should remain a prime suspect.

Therefore, although calculating errors might seem tedious at times, it is an essential scientific skill. In fact, dealing with experimental uncertainties is arguably the most important skill you will learn during these laboratory experiments.

There are many textbooks that explain how to deal with experimental errors in great details. For example, to write this section, we have used the two following textbooks:
- *Data Reduction and Error Analysis for the Physical Sciences, Authors: P.R. Bevington and D. K. Robinson, Editor: McGraw Hill.*
- *The Uncertainty in Physical Measurements, Author: P. Fornasini, Editor: Springer.*

For the purpose of the present labs, however, we only expect you to be familiar with and to be able to apply the rules outlined below.

6.1 CALCULATING EXPERIMENTAL ERRORS

When you measure a quantity (e.g. the mass of a plastic dinosaur), the value that you obtain may not be accurate, in other words it may differ from the true value of that quantity for a number of reasons.

- You may have made a mistake in your measurement or when reporting that measurement. These types of errors are called *illegitimate errors* and should be avoided by carefully performing and repeating experiments, by having your lab partner check on you when you are performing a measurement, and by taking good notes.

- The instrument you are using may not be properly calibrated, or you may be introducing a bias in your measurement because of the way you are reading your instrument (for example, if you do not take into account the presence of a meniscus when reading the level of a liquid, or if you do not take into account your reaction time when measuring the duration of an event). These types of errors are called *systematic errors*, and when they cannot be avoided, their presence should be recognized and taken into account as much as possible.

Introduction

- The precision of the instrument you are using for your measurement, and the precision of your reading of this instrument, will always be limited, introducing *random errors* in your measurements. These errors should be limited as much as possible, and the remaining error should be estimated (for example by taking into account the precision of your measuring instrument, often given by the manufacturer).

So how do you estimate the error associated with the value of a quantity you are measuring? There are basically two ways to proceed, and you should always use both, to check which one gives you the largest error. The error you want to keep is the largest error! <u>The last thing one wants to do when reporting the result of an experiment is to underestimate the experimental error associated with it, because it can lead to false conclusions</u> (for example, coming back to our Thode library murder mystery example, if you underestimate the error associated with the time of death you measured, you might wrongly rule out Miss Scarlet as a suspect; on the other hand, if you overestimate your error, then no wrong conclusion is reached).

1- <u>Direct evaluation of the experimental error</u>. If you know the precision of the instrument you are using, and if you think you are using the instrument optimally (no usage error, no reading error), then your experimental error should be equal to this precision. For example, if you are using a balance with a precision of 1 g, then the error associated with the mass you are measuring should be ± 1 g.

2- <u>Statistical evaluation of the experimental error</u>. If your experimental error is random (i.e. not systematic), then measuring the same value a number of times will return a number of slightly different values, and the average of these values should be very close to the real value. How close? To estimate this, you can calculate the standard deviation of your series of values (e.g. with Excel). If you have a large number of values (~ more than 5), then use the standard error, which is simply the standard deviation divided by the square root of the number of values you have measured. Note: You may have learned to calculate the average value, and to subtract that average value from the minimum and then the maximum value, and then to take the maximum (or average) of these two differences as the error. This is just an approximation of the standard deviation method, and although not incorrect, we recommend you use the standard deviation or standard error as your method of choice. On the other hand, you may have heard of more complex method to estimate errors (e.g. student's t-test, ANOVA...), which are refinements of the method outlined here.

Note 1:

When discussing errors, be aware that there is a difference between the terms "accuracy" (which refers to how close your measurement of a quantity is to the actual value of that quantity, and which is affected by illegitimate, systematic and random errors) and "precision" (which refers to how reproducible your measurements are, in other words how close a particular measurement of a quantity is to the average value you obtain for that quantity; precision is not affected by illegitimate or systematic errors, only by random errors).

Introduction

Note 2:

As you can see, there are several ways of calculating errors. Sometimes, there is no right or wrong way, just two (or more) different ways. What we would like you to do is: 1/ Always try to estimate your experimental error. 2/ Always explain how you have estimated this error. 3/ When in doubt chose the method that gives you the largest error.

6.2 PROPAGATING ERRORS

The result of combined measurements has an uncertainty due to the uncertainties in the individual measurements themselves. Imagine for example that you just measured the mass, m, and velocity, v, of a dinosaur, along with the errors δm and δv associated with these quantities. The quantity you are really interested in, though, is the momentum of this dinosaur, p, which you can easily calculate using the expression $p=mv$. But how can you estimate the error δp associated with p? In this section we explain how to do this, i.e. we describe how to combine uncertainties in order to obtain the uncertainty in a calculated result.

In the following:
- $x, y, z, u, w...$ are variables whose values you have determined experimentally.
- $q = f(x, ... z)$ is a quantity which can be calculated from x, y, z, etc... (for example, one may have $q = x/y$).
- δx is the <u>absolute</u> experimental error associated with x (i.e. we have $x \pm \delta x$). It is always positive and it has the same dimension as x (i.e. if x is in meters, so is δx).
- $\delta x / |x|$ is the <u>relative</u> error associated with x (it is dimensionless, and it can always be expressed as a % by just multiplying it by 100).

Our goal is to calculate δq, the <u>absolute</u> error associated with q. Note, however, that it is sometime easier to first calculate $\delta q/q$, the <u>relative</u> error associated with q, and then to obtain δq as $\delta q = q \times \delta q/q$.

6.2.1 General formula to propagate uncertainties

The most general method (sometimes referred to as the differentiation method) for determining the uncertainty of a quantity $q = f(x, ..., z)$ is to calculate the partial derivatives of the function f, and to use the formula:

$$\delta q = \left| \frac{\partial f}{\partial x} \right| \delta x + \cdots + \left| \frac{\partial f}{\partial z} \right| \delta z \qquad \text{Eq. 1}$$

This formula will work with **any** function. However, most of the calculations you will perform will involve only simple operations (addition, multiplication, square root, etc...) in which cases Eq. 1 can be greatly simplified. In practice, it is therefore enough that you remember how to deal with the specific examples listed below.

Introduction

> Addition and subtraction

If q consists of the sum and/or the difference of x, y, ..., z (ie., q = ± x ± ... ± z), then the **absolute** uncertainty of q is the **sum of the absolute** uncertainties:

$$\delta q = \delta x + \delta y + ... + \delta z \qquad \qquad \text{Eq. 3}$$

Example: You take two steps forward (lengths $L_1 = 56 \pm 1$ cm and $L_2 = 47 \pm 2$ cm) and one step backward ($L_3 = 52 \pm 1$ cm). In total, you have moved by a distance $L = L_1 + L_2 - L_3 = 51 \underline{\pm 4 \text{ cm}}$, since $\delta L = \delta L_1 + \delta L_2 + \delta L_3 = 4$ cm.

> Multiplication and division

If q consists of the product and/or the ratio of x, y, u, v, ... (i.e. q = x × y × .../u/v/ ...), then the **relative** uncertainty of q is the **sum of the relative** uncertainties:

$$\frac{\delta q}{|q|} = \frac{\delta x}{x} + \frac{\delta y}{|y|} + ... + \frac{\delta u}{|u|} + \frac{\delta v}{|v|} + ... \qquad \qquad \text{Eq. 4}$$

Example: Suppose that, when you watch TV, your heart beats every $\tau = 1.0 \pm 0.1$s. Then during an episode of Buffy the Vampire Slayer (duration: $T = 45 \pm 1$ min $= 2700 \pm 60$ s) your heart beats $N = T/\tau = 2700 \underline{\pm 400}$ times, since $\delta N = N \times (\delta T/T + \delta\tau/\tau) = 330$. (1 significant digit kept, only)

> Multiplication by _only a constant_

If q = ax, where a is a constant (that is a quantity which you know with infinite precision, i.e. $\delta a = 0$):

$$\delta q = a\delta x \qquad \qquad \text{Eq. 2}$$

Example: You measure the radius of a circle to be $R = 45 \pm 1$ cm. Then the diameter of this circle is $D = 2R = 90 \underline{\pm 2 \text{ cm}}$, since $\delta D = 2\delta R = 2$ cm.

> Powers

If $q = x^n$, where x has an uncertainty δx and the quantity n is known exactly, the **relative** uncertainty in q is given by:

$$\frac{\delta q}{|q|} = |n|\frac{\delta x}{|x|} \qquad \qquad \text{Eq. 5}$$

> Other

Other useful cases include **logarithms**: $q = \ln cx$, for which $\delta q = \delta x / |x|$ (note that for logarithms to base 10 it is necessary to convert to base e: $q = \log_{10} x = 0.43 \ln x$), **exponentials**: $q = e^x$, for which $\delta q = e^x \delta x$, and **Sine/Cosine functions**: $q = \sin \theta$, for which $\delta q = \cos \theta \; \delta\theta$ (note that $\delta\theta$ must be in radians).

Introduction

6.2.2 Adding uncertainties in quadrature

If all of the uncertainties are *independent* and *random* (ie. **not** systematic) then the uncertainties tend to partially cancel. Adding uncertainties using the above method can result in a final uncertainty that is unnecessarily large. This can be adjusted by adding the uncertainties in <u>quadrature</u>, according to the following:

> **General formula**

$$\delta q = \sqrt{\left(\left|\frac{\delta f}{\delta x}\right|\delta x\right)^2 + \ldots + \left(\left|\frac{\delta f}{\delta z}\right|\delta z\right)^2}$$

Eq. 6

> **Addition & subtraction**

$$\delta q = \sqrt{(\delta x)^2 + \ldots + (\delta z)^2}$$

Eq. 7

> **Multiplication & division**

$$\frac{\delta q}{|q|} = \sqrt{\left(\frac{\delta x}{|x|}\right)^2 + \left(\frac{\delta y}{|y|}\right)^2 + \ldots + \left(\frac{\delta u}{|u|}\right)^2 + \left(\frac{\delta v}{|v|}\right)^2 + \ldots}$$

Eq. 8

During the labs, you may choose whether or not to propagate uncertainties in quadrature (something which becomes easy when using a program like Excel). Just remember when writing your lab report that **you should always document** which approach you used and why.

12

Introduction

7. The correct use of significant digits

When solving textbook, LONCAPA and exam questions, you are usually not given uncertainty values. In those cases, when reporting a final numerical answer to the problem, the rule is that your answer should have only as many significant digits as the number with the lowest number of significant digits used for the calculation. For example, if you are asked to calculate the speed of a car which covers a distance $d = 52.7$ m in $t = 12$ s, then you should report the answer as $v = d/t = 4.4$ m/s (keeping only 2 significant digits, since t only has 2 significant digits).

During labs, however, you should always make the effort to calculate the uncertainties associated with your experimental results. And when reporting an experimental result, you should always mention both the **value of your results AND the associated uncertainty**. Furthermore, you should make sure that the value you report is expressed with the correct number of significant digits. As a first rule for undergraduate labs, you should keep only one significant digit for your absolute uncertainty. As a second rule, the last significant digit (that is the rightmost nonzero digit) of your reported value should be in the same decimal place as the last significant digit of the associated uncertainty. When you can calculate the value of the uncertainty, these rules take precedence over the simple rule enunciated in the first paragraph, which is valid only when you do not know the value of the uncertainty.

For example:

L = (1.12 ± 0.05) cm   is correct

L = (1.12354 ± 0.05) cm   is <u>incorrect</u> (the value of L has too many significant digits)

L = (1.1 ± 0.05) cm   is <u>incorrect</u> (the value of L does not have enough significant digits)

L = (1.12354 ± 0.05546) cm   is <u>incorrect</u> (the uncertainty has too many significant digits)

L = (1.124 ± 0.050) cm   is <u>incorrect</u> (the uncertainty and L have too many significant digits)

L = (1.12 ± 0.050) cm   is <u>incorrect</u> (the uncertainty has too many significant digits)

Finally, keep in mind that it is always a good idea to keep all your significant digits during intermediate calculations, and to truncate your results to the correct number of significant digits only when reporting your final result (this is to avoid round-off errors).

Introduction

8. Common uncertainty and significant digit problems

8.1 AVERAGES

Four students measure the length of an object and their results are as follows:

$$L_1 = 23.8 \text{ cm}, \quad L_2 = 24.0 \text{ cm}, \quad L_3 = 23.6 \text{ cm}, \quad L_4 = 23.9 \text{ cm}, \quad L_5 = 23.7 \text{ cm}$$

a) What is the average measurement?

$$L_{avg} = (L_1 + L_2 + L_3 + L_4 + L_5)/n = (23.8 + 24.0 + 23.6 + 23.9 + 23.7)/5 = 119.9/5 = 23.80 \text{ cm}$$

b) What is the range of measured values?

$$R = L_{max} - L_{min} = 24.0 - 23.6 = 0.4 \text{ cm}$$

c) What is the absolute uncertainty?

$$\delta L = R/n = (L_{max} - L_{min})/5 = 0.4/5 = \pm 0.08 \text{ cm}$$

d) What is the final answer?

$$\underline{L_{avg} = 23.80 \pm 0.08 \text{ cm}}$$

8.2 MULTIPLICATION INCLUDING A CONSTANT

Calculate the uncertainty in the area of a circle, whose radius is:

$$R = 9.8 \pm 0.9 \text{ cm}$$

Area of a circle:

$$A = \pi R^2 = \pi (9.8)^2 = 301.5656 \text{ cm}^2$$

Relative uncertainty of R:

$$\delta R/R = 0.9/9.8 = 0.0918 = 9.18\%$$

Relative uncertainty of π:

$$\delta \pi/\pi = 0$$

Relative uncertainty of Area:

$$\delta A/A = \delta R/R + \delta R/R + \delta \pi/\pi = 0.0918 + 0.0918 + 0 = 0.1836 = 18.36\%$$

Absolute uncertainty of Area:

$$\delta A = A (\delta R/R + \delta R/R + \delta \pi/\pi) = (301.5656 \text{ cm}^2)(0.1836) = 55.37 \text{ cm}$$

$$\delta A = 60 \text{ cm (Absolute uncertainty can only have \textbf{1 significant digit})}$$

14

Final answer:

$$A = 301.5656 \pm 30 \text{ cm}^2 = \underline{300 \pm 30 \text{ cm}^2}$$

(The final answer must **match the decimal place of your uncertainty**. In this case our uncertainty was in the tens decimal place, so our final answer must be rounded to the tens decimal place as well.)

8.3 Multiplication & Division with multiple uncertainties

An object falls from a height of ($h = 30 \pm 3$ cm) in a time ($t = 8.3 \pm 0.5$ s). What is the velocity?

Velocity:

$$V = 2h/t = 2*(30 \text{ cm})/(8.3 \text{ s}) = 7.23 \text{ cm/s}$$

Relative uncertainty of velocity:

$$\delta V/V = \delta(2)/2 + \delta(h)/h + \delta(t)/t = 0 + 3/30 + 0.5/8.3 = 0.1602 = 16.02\%$$

Absolute uncertainty of velocity:

$$\delta V = V (\delta(2)/2 + \delta(h)/h + \delta(t)/t) = (7.23)(0.1602) = 1.159 = 2 \text{ cm/s}$$

Final answer:

$$V = 7.23 \pm 2 \text{ cm/s} = \underline{7 \pm 2 \text{ cm/s}}$$

8.4 Addition and Subtraction with multiple uncertainties

Find the perimeter of a box whose length and width are as follows:

$$L = 23.4 \pm 0.3 \text{ cm} \qquad W = 11.34 \pm 0.09 \text{ cm}$$

Perimeter:

$$P = 2(L+W) = L + L + W + W = 23.4 + 23.4 + 11.34 + 11.34 = 69.48 \text{ cm}$$

Absolute uncertainty:

$$\delta P = \delta L + \delta L + \delta W + \delta W = 0.3 + 0.3 + 0.09 + 0.09 = 0.78 = 0.8$$

Final answer:

$$P = 69.48 \pm 0.8 \text{ cm} = \underline{69.5 \pm 0.8 \text{ cm}}$$

Introduction

9. Pre-labs

Before each lab, you will have to complete a pre-lab. Each pre-lab consists in a few questions related to the topic of the associated laboratory experiment or to the experimental or analysis techniques that will be used in this lab.

We ask you to complete a pre-lab in order to make sure that you have already given some thoughts and assimilated some key concepts used in the lab. You might not know the answers to the pre-lab questions off-hand, and we encourage you to research the right answer by reading your textbook or other sources, or if necessary by discussing the pre-lab questions with other students or TAs. The important thing is that by the time you fill in the answers, you feel that you understand what you are doing.

You need complete your pre-lab before going to the lab. You will not be accepted in the lab if you don't have yet completed your pre-lab.

You must bring the prelab graph with you to the lab so it can be marked by your TA. Either printed, or saved on your computer is acceptable.

10. Lab report Breakdown

Your lab reports should be typed (12 point fonts, single spaced) and structured as a scientific paper. It should contain the following sections (clearly labeled):

1. An **introduction**, which explains the scientific context of your experiment. This introduction should be clear and concise, and it should show that you understand the broad context of your experiment. Do not forget to correctly cite any external source of information you use for your introduction (and later for your discussion), including the laboratory manual.

2. A **hypothesis**, which should be only one sentence, in which you clearly explain what question you are trying to answer with the experiment you are presenting.

3. A **method** section, where you explain your experimental strategy. You should say what your experiment consisted of, giving enough experimental details for another student doing the same lab to be able to reproduce your experiments, and always trying to justify why you have done things this way rather than another. Methods how you reduced the sources of error are essential.

4. A **results** section where you report on what you have measured, and explain the data analysis you have performed on your data. This section contains one or more graphs or tables that summarize in a condensed and readable way the results of your experiments. In this section, refrain from commenting on the significance of your data.

5. A **discussion**, where you compare your results to what one would expect given available theories or given previous experiments performed by others, where you comment on the significance of your data (discussing whether your results prove or disprove your hypothesis, at which point an estimate of the uncertainty of your measurements is essential), and where you discuss how your results may or may not support your hypothesis.

6. A **conclusion**, where you summarize your results very quickly, and where you clearly indicate whether your data indicates that your hypothesis was false or true. You must finish this section by suggesting a better experiment or a better way to perform the experiment in order improve or further your hypothesis. This conclusion should be very short, a few sentences at most.

Your repost must also contain:

1. A **cover sheet** with your name and other relevant information (see example on the next page, a template can be downloaded from the website).

2. A blank **feedback form**, which your TA will use for marking and return with your report. You can download this feedback form from the course website.

Remember that your TA will have only ~15 to 30 min to read and evaluate your report, so make sure you keep them happy by writing clearly and concisely.

Also note that plagiarism will be very seriously dealt with, resulting in a mark of zero for a particular lab, all the labs, or the course, depending on the offense. Discussing results and ideas with lab partners or fellow students is encouraged, but when it comes to writing your report, every word should be your own.

Introduction

11. How to analyze Data

The proper analysis of data is vital to a proper scientific report. This means knowing how to apply correct uncertainty and significant digits to any measured values. Sections 6 and 7 of the lab manual outline the rules of both, and we will be applying those rules in this section.

11.1 RESULTS

The results section is a collection of all the relevant data you have collected; including tables, graphs and sample calculations.

11.1.1 Tables

On the course website, you are given an excel template outlining all the measurements you need to complete during the lab. The whole template should never be in your lab report. The tables in the report are of <u>relevant</u> data only.

Lab #1: Vitruvian Man Excel Template

	Trial #	Notes	Length (cm) L1	Error (cm) δL1	Average Length (cm)	Error (cm)	Length (cm) L2	Error (cm) δL2	Average Length (cm)	Error(cm)	Ratio r = L1/L2	Absolute error δr	Relative error δr/r
Subject 1	Trial 1												
	Trial 2												
	Trial 3												
Subject 2	Trial 1												
	Trial 2												
	Trial 3												
Subject 3	Trial 1												
	Trial 2												
	Trial 3												
Subject 4	Trial 1												
	Trial 2												
	Trial 3												
Subject 5	Trial 1												
	Trial 2												
	Trial 3												
Subject 6	Trial 1												
	Trial 2												
	Trial 3												

X   This whole template is not acceptable in a report, and will result in a large deduction of marks. There is a lot of unnecessary information here that should not be in your final report.

Introduction

Lab #1: Vitruvian Man Table of Relevant Data

Average Foot Length (L)	δL	Average Height (H)	δH	Ratio (R)	δR
19.8	0.5	140	2	7.1	0.3
23.5	0.5	169	2	7.2	0.2
27.4	0.5	183	2	6.7	0.2
24.5	0.5	171	2	7.0	0.2
22.3	0.5	157	2	7.0	0.2
22.9	0.5	160	2	7.0	0.2

✓ This table only outlines the necessary data to discuss validity of hypothesis

11.1.2 Scientific Graphs

You will always need to include at least 1 graph in your lab report. This graph must include:

- Title
- Axis labels (with units)
- Error bars on both X and Y axis
- Line of best fit (relationship will always be linear)
- Equation of the trend line (with uncertainty on the slope and y-intercept, and R^2)

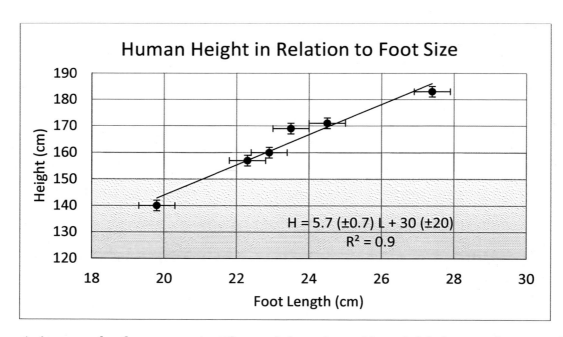

Figure 1: An example of a proper scientific graph featuring a title, axis labels, error bars, trend line equation with uncertainty, and the R^2 value.

Introduction

11.1.2.1 Uncertainty on slope and y-intercept

The uncertainty of both the slope and y-intercept are necessary to confirm or deny your hypothesis. Not including either will result in a major loss of marks to both your results section and the discussion. The method to find these values id outlined below.

11.1.2.1.1 The max/min slope method

This method uses the error bars to determine the steepest and shallowest line that can fit through your data. With these values, in comparison with the line of best fit, you can easily find the uncertainty on the slope and the y-intercept.

Best Fit trend line

To the line of best fit, use the linear trend line option on your graph in excel.

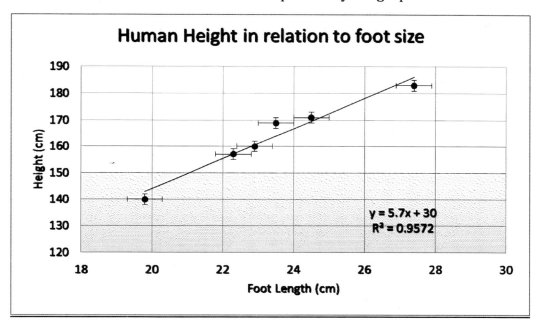

Best fit slope = 5.7   Best fit y-int = 30 cm

Maximum slope trend line

To get the steepest line that fits through your data, try connecting the most right part of the error bar on your lowest data point, to the most left part of your highest data point; see below. If the edge is a suspected outlier in your data, try the next furthest point.

Introduction

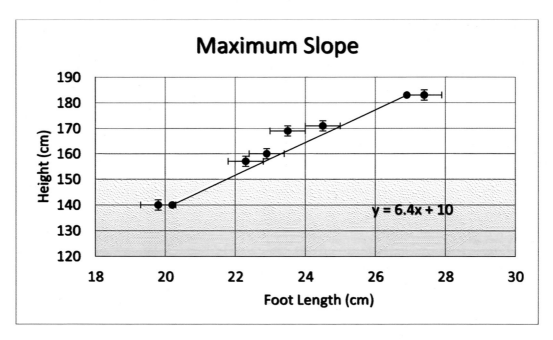

Now calculate the slope and y-intercept of this line, and label them as max slope, and min y-intercept.

        Max slope = 6.4   Min y-int = 10 cm

Minimum slope

To get the shallowest line that fits through your data, try connecting the most left part of the error bar on your lowest data point, to the most right part of your highest data point; see below. If the edge is a suspected outlier in your data, try the next furthest point.

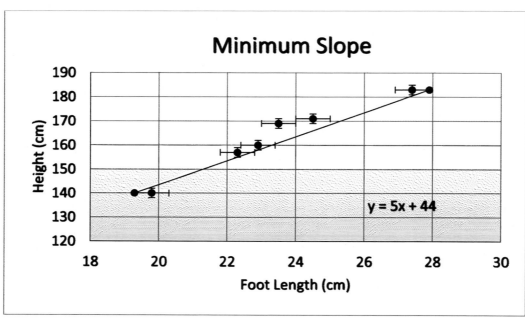

Introduction

Now calculate the slope and y-intercept of this line, and label them as min slope, and max y-intercept.

Min slope = 5   Max y-int = 44 cm

Uncertainty on line of best fit

To get the uncertainty of slope, take your max/min values of slope, and calculate the largest difference between them and the best fit slope.

Uncertainty of slope:

Max slope – Best fit slope = 6.4 – 5.7 = 0.7

Best fit slope – Min slope = 5.7 – 5 = 0.7

The larger difference is 0.7, so this value is the uncertainty on the slope.

Slope = 5.7 ± 0.7

Note: Notice the proper significant digits.

To get the uncertainty of the y-intercept, take your max/min values of y-intercept, and calculate the largest difference between them and the best fit intercept.

Uncertainty of y-intercept:

Max y-int – Best fit y-int = 44 – 30 = 14

Best fit y-int – Min y-int = 30 – 10 = 20

The larger difference is 20, so this value is the uncertainty on the y-intercept.

Y-intercept: 30 ± 20

Note: Notice the proper significant digits.

On the final graph in your report

The uncertainty values will need to be added in by hand to the best fit trend line equation, and the slope and y-intercept will need to be adjusted to the proper significant digits.

Best fit trend line equation on your final graph should read:

H = 5.7 (± 0.7) L + 30 (± 20)

11.1.2.2 Linear Correlation (R² Value)

Whether two variables are <u>linearly correlated</u> can be assessed by considering the correlation coefficient, R, or the square of the correlation coefficient, R^2. This coefficient gives a measure of the linear relationship between the two variables plotted on your chart. If R^2 is close to 1, you can consider that there is a strong linear correlation between your two variables. To illustrate this concept, consider the examples below (found at http://mathworld.wolfram.com/CorrelationCoefficient.html).

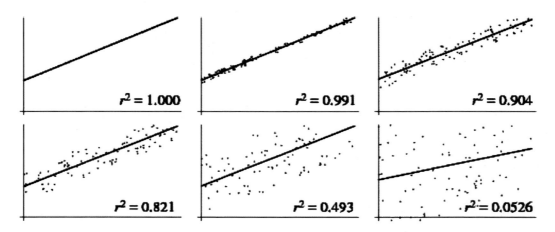

An R^2 value above 0.8 is considered a good correlation. Less than 0.5 is a bad correlation. You must consider both parameters of the linear fit and the R-squared value you obtain for your data and must mention in "results" what type of linear correlation results between your data set.

You can briefly discuss the implications of your linear correlation in the discussion, but **the R² value is not a significant contributor to whether your results agree or disagree with your hypothesis.**

To understand what the R^2 value means to a linear graph, check out the web game:

guessthecorrelation.com

11.1.2.1.2 Excel toolbox add-on for large sets of data (Lab 4)

To obtain an error on the values of the slope and intercept when you have **more than 10 points**, you will need to perform a linear regression analysis using Excel Analysis Tool Pack. To do so:

- Select Data Analysis -> Regression Analysis from the Tools Menu.
- As "X Range" chose the cells corresponding to your first data set
- As "Y Range" chose the cells corresponding to your second data set

Introduction

- If you included the labels in your X and Y range check the "Labels" box.
- Chose any empty cell on your workbook as the "Output Range" (this is where Excel will write the result of the linear regression analysis)
- Click OK and the result of the regression analysis will appear.

For a step by step video tutorial, check out the following link (starting at 8:40 for regression analysis):

http://calcscience.uwe.ac.uk/w2/am/ExcelTuts/Excel2007/RegAnalysisA/RegAnalysisA.html

11.1.3 Sample Calculations

You must include in your results section any key calculations you have done, including uncertainty calculations. One example per calculation is sufficient. All your work should not be included.

11.2 DISCUSSING RESULTS

The discussion is the most important part of the lab report, and is worth the most marks. This is the section where you discuss your results, and confirm or reject your hypothesis.

11.2.1 Agreement of hypothesis to results

Your hypothesis is a very direct statement of a relationship; for example: A person's height is 6 times their foot length. In your results section you will have this ratio calculated, with an uncertainty. To prove or reject this hypothesis you need to directly compare your result with your hypothesis.

Example:

Hypothesis: $H = 6 * L$

Result: $H = 6.5 \ (\pm 0.4) * L$

The hypothesis is disproven because 6 does not lie in the range 6.5 ± 0.4.

Do the following values agree with the hypothesis?

a) 6.5 ± 0.5

b) 5.8 ± 0.1

c) 6.9 ± 0.8

Answer: a) Yes b) No c) No

24

Introduction

Agreement is a Yes/No statement. There are no maybes or approximately. If you say that your result was "close to" the hypothesis, or get the agreement wrong you will lose 50% of the discussion marks. This is because you have included of all the significant uncertainties, so if the hypothesis is true, it absolutely must lie within your result uncertainty. If it does not, then your results do not agree with the hypothesis.

The way these labs are designed, your result will often not agree with the hypothesis due to simplification of the theory/equation under investigation. Not agreeing with the hypothesis does not make your science wrong and will not lose you marks. Lying about your results and forcing an answer will make you lose many marks, and often result in a failed lab grade.

Show all your steps, and describe explicitly how your results agree/disagree with the hypothesis. This means that your result MUST have an uncertainty.

Note: the R^2 value is not a significant contributor to whether your results agree or disagree with your hypothesis. The analysis of the slope AND y-intercept are the most significant.

11.2.2 Error analysis

The next part of the discussion is stating many of the significant errors that were out of your control. For example, the largest group you will work with is 6 people. Sample size is a source of error out of your control, for certain relevant experiments.

Ruler measurement, reading things by eye and all around human error should never be talked about in this section. You will lose marks if it is. This is because when you design your method, you attach an uncertainty to your measured values that includes this error. Therefore it is already incorporated in your final answer.

11.2.3 Further Analysis

The last part of the discussion, put your experimental results in broader terms. Describe exactly what you would need to get more accurate results. This means specific examples. Stating "more accurate equipment" is much too broad. If you would need more sensitive technology, what machine specifically.

25

Introduction

12. Sample cover sheet

Lab #1: Lab Report Title

First names: Frodo, Samwise

Last names: Baggins, Gamgee

Student number: 001234567

Email Address: bagginsf@theshire.me

gamgees@theshire.me

Class: Physics 1A03

Lab section: L01 (Monday)

Lab partners: Peregrin Took

Meriadoc Brandybuck

Experiment date: Jan. 12, 2017

Report hand in date: Jan. 19, 2017

Introduction

13. Lab Report Marking Scheme

Each of your lab reports will be marked out of 100 according to the following scheme:

	Lab #1	Lab #2	Lab #3	Lab #4
Presentation	10	10	10	10
Introduction	15	14	15	15
Hypothesis	5	5	5	5
Method	15	15	15	15
Results	15	16	13	20
Graphs/Tables	15	15	17	15
Discussion	20	20	20	15
Conclusion	5	5	5	5
TOTAL /100				

14. Feedback Form

The feedback form contains a breakdown of each section listed above, with a list of common errors in each. The marking TA will circle any areas you need to improve on for the next lab report. This rubric does not necessarily cover all the possible qualities or weaknesses of a lab report, but it will help you understand what is expected from you in order to fulfill expectations and get good marks on your lab reports. Note that you may also get a mark between different categories.

The appropriate Feedback form must be attached to the end of each report, or you will lose marks. Each feedback form can be downloaded from the course website.

If you get an "Unacceptable" rating in any of the categories above, your TA will notify your course instructor.

Also, remember that we expect you to improve over the course of the semester. So take into account the feedback of the TAs, as marking will become stricter as the semester progresses.

27

Introduction

Part II: Experiments

You will perform 4 different laboratory experiments as part of this course. For each of these labs, you should expect to do the following:

Before the lab.
We do expect you to be <u>prepared</u> when you come to the lab. This is important because it allows you to complete you experiment and analysis faster, to ask meaningful questions during the lab, to contribute fully to the discussions with your lab partner(s), and to get a deeper understanding of the physical concepts underlying your experiment. In order to prepare for the lab:

1) **Read the instructions** provided for that lab beforehand.

2) **Complete the pre-lab** (which opens on the course website a couple days before your lab). You will need to <u>hand in your completed graph</u> when you come to the lab.

3) **Download the excel template** from the course website, to bring to the lab to record and analyze your data.

During the lab.
There will be a 10-15 min demo at the start of all labs to briefly familiarize you with the apparatus available. You should spend the next 15-20 mins with your partner/group to discuss and develop a hypothesis and method. You will then have 2 ½ hours left to collect your data, and start analyzing.

You are encouraged to discuss with and ask questions to other students and TA, but <u>you must perform your own analysis</u>.

Before leaving the lab.
1) **All results are recorded** in the excel template.

2) **Email the excel template** as a group to your TA, indicating your name and the name of your group in the body of the email.

This spreadsheet might be marked and/or be used to compile the data acquired by all students to prepare a wrap-up session. Also, sending this completed or half-completed spreadsheet before the end of the lab session will be taken as the proof that you did attend the lab.

After the lab
Write a lab report, and make sure to return it in the **1A03 Drop Box found outside of BSB-B110,** within one week of the lab session (or according to your TA instructions).

28

Lab #1: The Vitruvian Man

1. Introduction

1.1 A Scenario

It's a cold day in January, and your best friend Bob is freezing. Since you are such an awesome friend, you decide to knit Bob a onesie for his upcoming birthday. You just so happen to know a number of his measurements; all except for his height. But you are equipped with science, so you know just what to do.

You run to Thode library trying to find information about the Vitruvian man. This famous drawing by Leonardo da Vinci represents a man with outstretched arms, inscribed in a square and in a circle. By reading the corresponding Wikipedia entry (en.wikipedia.org/wiki/Vitruvian_Man), you learn that da Vinci was inspired by the work of a roman architect, Vitruvius Pollo. In his treatise, *Ten Books on Architecture*, Pollo had enunciated a number of rules concerning the proportions of the human body, which da Vinci followed and outlined in his drawing.

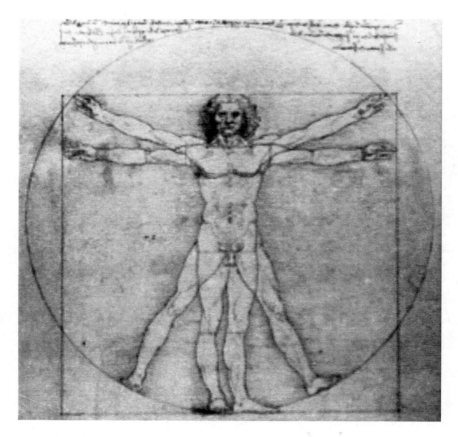

en.wikipedia.org/wiki/Vitruvian_Man

Lab #1   The Vitruvian Man

The following passage stands out to you:

"For the human body is so designed by nature that the face, from the chin to the top of the forehead and the lowest roots of the hair, is a tenth part of the whole height; the open hand from the wrist to the tip of the middle finger is just the same; the head from the chin to the crown is an eighth, and with the neck and shoulder from the top of the breast to the lowest roots of the hair is a sixth; from the middle of the breast to the summit of the crown is a fourth. If we take the height of the face itself, the distance from the bottom of the chin to the underside of the nostrils is one third of it; the nose from the underside of the nostrils to a line between the eyebrows is the same; from there to the lowest roots of the hair is also a third, comprising the forehead. The length of the foot is one sixth of the height of the body; of the forearm, one fourth; and the breadth of the breast is also one fourth. The other members, too, have their own symmetrical proportions, and it was by employing them that the famous painters and sculptors of antiquity attained to great and endless renown."

Vitruvius Pollo, Ten Books on Architecture, translated from latin by M. H. Morgan, Harvard University Press.

Gathering a group of your peers, you develop an experiment to determine Bob's height, without his knowledge.

1.2 Bob's measurements

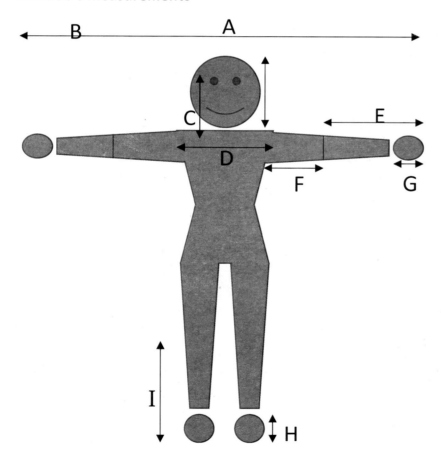

A. 171 cm
B. 21 cm
C. 28 cm
D. 43 cm
E. 45 cm
F. 22 cm
G. 17 cm
H. See next page
I. 41 cm

30

Lab #1   **The Vitruvian Man**

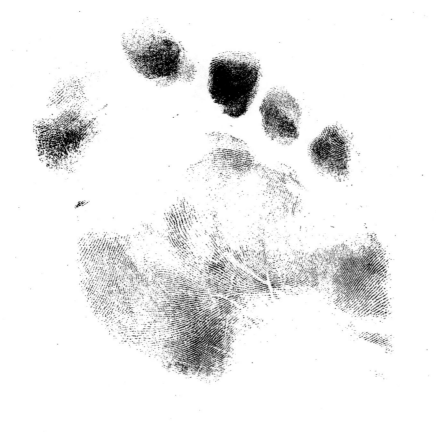

Reproduction (to scale) of Bob's footprint

Lab #1   The Vitruvian Man

2. PURPOSE OF THE LAB (GIVEN FOR LAB #1 ONLY)

Given all the measurements of a subject, except for their height, you must find this height through science! This means testing out the Vitruvian man model, and seeing if it's valid.

2.1 Available tools:

- Measuring tape
- Meter sticks (and double meter sticks)
- Masking tape
- Leveling app on phone

2.2 Useful Information gathered from Introduction:

A. Length of the outspread arms is equal to the height of a man
B. Below the chin to the top of the head is one-eighth of the height of a man
C. Above the chest to the hairline is one-seventh of the height of a man.
D. Maximum width of the shoulders is a quarter of the height of a man.
E. Distance from the elbow to the tip of the hand is a quarter of the height of a man.
F. Distance from the elbow to the armpit is one-eighth of the height of a man.
G. Length of the hand is one-tenth of the height of a man.
H. Foot length is one-sixth of the height of a man.
I. Below the foot to below the knee is a quarter of the height of a man.

All of these are valid ways to get the height of the subject. As a group of 6, choose which experiment you would like to perform.

3. HYPOTHESIS

After choosing an experiment, you now should spend time as a group writing your hypothesis. Your hypothesis needs to briefly and effectively state what theory you are testing, and specifically what equation. For Lab #1, fill in the blanks below:

"According to the Vitruvian man model, the height of a person is __4__ times the length of their _____. This is expressed mathematically in the equation:
elbow to tip of hand.

$$H = 4 \times L$$

elbow to tip of hand[1]

Where H is the height of a person, and L is the length of their _____. "

Note: "..." is the number corresponding to the ratio. Do not forget to fill the appropriate number in.

32

Lab #1   **The Vitruvian Man**

4. METHOD

The method section is completely up to your group to create. Minimizing the uncertainty in your measurements is the most important aspect.

Remember:

- How will you decide the uncertainty attached to the height of a person? Their head is curved.

- Where are you taking your measurements from? Is this consistent across all the members in your group?

- Is ±0.5 mm enough of an uncertainty for ruler measurements? *(Hint: No, it is not.)*

- If you take a measurement on a ruler, there is a start and end to that measurement. Both sides have uncertainty. Do not forget to add them together.

5. REPORT INFORMATION

In pairs, write a <u>short</u> report (you should aim for 4 pages maximum, plus references and title page) including: an introduction providing background, a clear statement of your hypothesis, a description of your experimental method (with a figure), a short description of your results (including a graph and table), and a discussion and conclusion. Refer to Part I: Chapter 10 of the lab manual to learn how to analyze the data you have collected, and write a good report.

Don't forget in your results section to calculate Bob's height!

"Bob's height is _____ ± _____."

In your discussion, talk about the accuracy of this calculation.

Return your completed report to the 1AA3 drop boxes outside BSB B110, or as per your TA's instruction. Check Avenue announcements.

Lab #1   **The Vitruvian Man**

5.1 What is being marked?

- Introduction, Hypothesis, Method, Results, Discussion, Conclusion, Presentation, and graphs/tables

Must have resources/sources cited, or you are committing academic dishonesty. This includes and figures you use that you didn't make yourself.

Presentation /10
- Neatness of report
- Clear titles
- Completely typed (including equations)
- Proper spacing of report (no blank spaces) and placement of diagrams (no more than ½ page)
- Proper order of topics
- Report bound properly (stapled!)
- Title page in the format in your lab manual (page. 26)
- Feedback form attached

Introduction /15
- Introduce the history of the model, and the physics.
- Must have an equation, and number the equation.
- Not too long/short. Be clear and concise.
- Check for spelling errors and grammatical errors
- Source the topics you introduce (listed at the end of report. Must have at least 3)
- NOT copied from manual, but should use the manual as one of your sources

Hypothesis /5
- Write in hypothesis form; write concisely and be clear.
- An equation must be used, either referenced from the introduction or stated here
- Max 5 sentences (typically 1-2 each). Check for spelling/grammar

Method /15
- Step-by-step process of how you performed the experiment in sentences
- Includes at least 1 figure, with figure number and caption
- Include how you minimized uncertainty and how you decided on an uncertainty
- Should be able to replicate your entire process from reading this section

Results /15
- Include sentences connecting results to method
- State results (no discussion of results, that belongs in the discussion)
- Show sample calculations of every equation you used and the uncertainty calculations for those values
- Number relevant equations and tables/graphs so you can reference them in discussion
- **Make sure you have proper significant figures, units and uncertainty on all values**

34

Lab #1   **The Vitruvian Man**

Graphs & Tables /15

- Belongs in your results section
- Titles, axis labels, units, significant figures, figure numbers & captions
- Proper scale of data
    - Not lodged in a corner of the graph, doesn't have to start at (0,0).
- Error bars (x and y)
- Show best fit relationship
    - Has a linear trend line
    - Relates to hypothesis equation. Must be able to get relevant information from the slope and y-intercept.
    - Equation shown on graph, with an uncertainty on slope and y-int and an R^2 value.
- Use proper colours and symbols so your graph can be easily read

Discussion /20

- The most important section of the lab report.
- Restate your hypothesis
- State whether your end results agreed/disagreed with your hypotheses
    - Compare slope and y-intercept to your hypothesis equation, <u>using uncertainty</u>.
    - Do they both agree? Does only 1?
- Then discuss
    - Is there something obviously wrong with the model? What is it?
    - What does you R^2 value say about your trendline?
    - Discuss any graphs/tables you put in your results section
    - What should the y-intercept be? What does having a y-int mean?
    - How does Bob's height look to you? Does your uncertainty seam reasonable?
- Error analysis: What are the main sources of error? Don't say "human error"; be specific.
    - Are statistics relevant in this lab?
    - Look for the big sources of error.
        - What measurement is most likely going wrong?
        - What specifically would make your measurements better?
    - <u>Do not</u> list sources of error you have already taken into account with uncertainty. They are not sources of error if you have already included their effect in your final answer (ie. Uncertainty).

Conclusion /5

- Restate your hypothesis <u>and the end results</u> (with uncertainty and units).
- Further investigation
- 1 paragraph, ~5 sentences
- Nothing new is introduced

Total: /100

Lab #2   Rotating Dinosaurs

2. LAB #2: ROTATIONAL MOTION

1. INTRODUCTION
1.1 Moment of inertia

From Newton's second law, $F = ma$, the mass of an object determines how effective a given force will be in producing linear acceleration (i.e. accelerating the object in the direction of the force). In a rotational system, <u>moment of inertia</u> is the exact analogue of mass in a linear translational system. That is, the moment of inertia I of an object determines how effective a given torque will be in producing an angular acceleration. I depends not only on the mass of the object, but also on <u>how the mass is distributed</u> with respect to the axis of rotation.

We can always imagine digitizing our object into a 3-dimensional grid of tiny cubes. The mass of the ith cube is m_i. The moment of inertia of the entire object is:

$$I = \sum_i m_i r_i^2 \qquad (1)$$

Where r_i is the perpendicular distance of the ith mass from the axis of rotation. Of course for a non-ideal object (e.g. a dinosaur) it would be very complicated to calculate the moment of inertia in this manner.

Lab #2   Rotating Dinosaurs

1.2 For your Report Introduction

2. Find out who introduced the idea of angular momentum, and what they used it for (Paragraph 1)
3. Define what angular momentum is and the equation you are studying in this lab. (Paragraph 2)

The equation you are studying in this lab is:
$$I = mR^2 \qquad (2)$$

Where I is the moment of Inertia, m is the mass (of the weight on the crossbar, in kilograms) and R is the radius of the masses from the axis of rotation.

Remember you must have 3 sources (the lab manual can count as 1).

2. EQUIPMENT

- Weights with different masses
- Scale
- Stop-watches (or phone)
- Meter sticks
- Apparatus to measure moment of inertia:

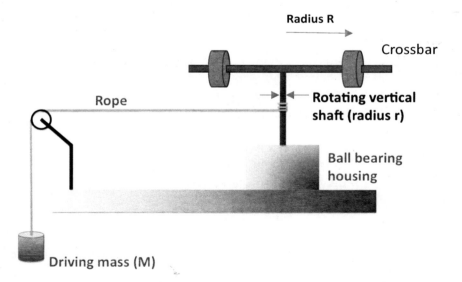

Figure 2: *Experimental set-up used to measure the moment of inertia of masses on the crossbar.*

Lab #2 — Rotating Dinosaurs

The apparatus to measure moment of inertia consists of a vertical rotating shaft **(radius r = 6.6 ± 0.2 mm)** and a horizontal crossbar to which one can attach different weights (see Fig. 2 above). To measure the moment of inertia of a mass we will apply a torque to the system and observe the resulting angular motion. The torque is provided by a driving mass attached to a cord wound around the shaft. By measuring the **time t_0** the **driving mass M** takes to fall a **height h**, we can determine the moment of inertia of the rotating system (the corresponding equations are detailed in section 6).

3. Hypothesis

Spend ~10-15 mins among your group deciding on the wording of your hypothesis. Think about the first lab and how that hypothesis was phrased. When you are done, call your TA over to make sure you are on the right track.

Hint: The equation of focus for this lab is that of a point mass:

$$I = mR^2$$

Where I is the total moment of inertia, m is the mass on the crossbar, and R is the distance away the masses are from the axis of rotation.

4. Method (in groups of 2)

In order to calculate the moment of inertia of the masses on the crossbar, we need to calibrate out equipment. This means we are going to calculate the moment of inertia of the apparatus itself, without any masses on the crossbar. This value is called **I_0**.

Knowing I_0, we can then put masses on the crossbar, and do the experiment again, measuring the total moment of inertia, **I_T**, of the whole apparatus with masses on it.

If we want to compare the masses on the crossbar to point masses, we need to find their moment of inertia, **I_m**. Since we know the whole moment of inertia, and the moment of inertia of the crossbar apparatus, this is a simple subtraction problem.

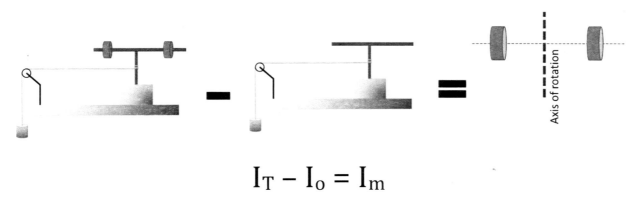

$$I_T - I_0 = I_m$$

Once we have I_m, we can compare it to our hypothesis, equation 2, and see if it agrees.

Lab #2   **Rotating Dinosaurs**

4.1 Uncertainty of time

Open the excel template, and click on tab #1. There is a section at the top to calculate the uncertainty in time. This is measuring your reaction time, which you can use as the uncertainty in all of your time measurements.

Step 1: Pick a goal time, recommended 3 seconds

Step 2: Try to stop the stopwatch at exactly this goal time

Step 3: Repeat at least 4 more times

Step 4: Take the average time

Step 5: Find the biggest difference from your trials to this average (this is the uncertainty)

Step 6: Adjust the significant digits so uncertainty only has 1

4.2 Calibration of equipment

You will first do a calibration experiment to measure I_0, the calibration moment of inertia, and to familiarize yourself with the instrumentation (this part should take you ~30 min).

Determine I_0 (moment of inertia of your instrument without any weight on the crossbar):

- Release the driving mass, M, and measure the time, t_0, it takes to fall a measured distance, h (about 75 cm).
- Repeat this trial 5 times to ensure you have an accurate value of t_0.
- Calculate the final velocity of the driving mass, v, using the average value you measured for t_0. Then calculate the final angular velocity of the shaft, ω, using the values you calculated for v and r (the equations you need to do these calculations are derived and shown in section 6).
- Calculate the initial energy of the system, which is equal to the potential energy of the driving mass (E_{pot}), and the final translational kinetic energy of the system (K_{trans}). Then obtain the rotational kinetic energy of the system, K_{rot}, using the principle of conservation of energy (see section 6).
- Finally, calculate I_0 from the value of K_{rot}, using the expression of the rotational kinetic energy (given in section 6).

Before going on, check with a TA that your value of I_0 is correct.

Lab #2   Rotating Dinosaurs

4.3 Total moment of inertia of crossbar

Use the same method as the calibration, calculate the moment of inertia of a pair of weights at varying radius, R, from the axis of rotation (see figure 2). You must make sure the two weights have the same mass and are placed on the crossbar at an equal distance to the shaft on opposite sides for balance.

Use the following R values:

14.54

15 cm, 12 cm, 10cm, 7 cm, 4 cm, 2 cm.

Note: "R" is the radius of the masses on the crossbar. While "r" is the radius of the shaft given in the equipment section.

You MUST measure the total mass you put on the crossbar. Weigh them now.

<u>Total Mass on the cross bar</u>

__0.03646__ kg (4 Wingnuts) + ___0.2___ kg (2 masses) = ___0.23646___ kg (total)

This is the value your slope should theoretically be if you plot I vs. R^2. Note the units.

5. REPORT INFORMATION

In pairs, write a short report (you should aim for 5 pages of text maximum, plus title page, figures and references).

Your methods and results section should have two parts: In the first part explaining the calibration, the second part explaining the moment of inertia of the crossbar.

Refer to Part I: Chapter 10 of the lab manual to learn how to analyze the data you have collected, and write a good report.

Results section must have sample calculations of:

Error in time, height, Error in height, v, ∂v, ω, $\partial \omega$, E_{pot}, ∂E_{pot}, E_{trans}, ∂E_{trans}, K_{rot}, ∂K_{rot}, I_o or I_t, ∂I, I_m, ∂I_m

Return your completed report to the 1AA3 drop boxes outside BSB B110, or as per your TA's instruction. Check Avenue announcements.

Lab #2   **Rotating Dinosaurs**

6. EQUATIONS OF MOTION

In this experiment the gravitational potential energy of a falling mass is converted into the translational kinetic energy of the driving mass and the rotational kinetic energy of the system. The conservation of energy principle requires the initial total energy of the system to be equal to its total final energy (provided frictional forces are negligible).

To calculate initial and final energy we need to know the initial and final conditions for the system. Initially, the system is at rest ($v_0 = 0$, $\omega_0 = 0$) and the driving mass is placed at a height h. To calculate v, the final velocity of the driving mass, from t, the time it takes for M to fall through h, we use the constant acceleration formulae: $v = v_0 + at$ and $v^2 = v_0^2 + 2ah$ (with $v_0 = 0$ in this case) to obtain:

$$v = \frac{2h}{t} \tag{3}$$

And since the string wound around the shaft has the same speed as the driving mass M, the final angular velocity of the platform is:

$$\omega = \frac{v}{r} \tag{4}$$

Where r is the radius of the shaft.

Initially, that is just before the system is released, the system is at rest, so the kinetic energy of the system is 0. Thus the initial energy of the system is equal to its potential energy:

$$E_{pot} = Mgh \tag{5}$$

Where the final (lowest) position of the **driving mass M** has been taken to be the zero point for potential energies.

At the end of the motion, that is just when the driving mass hits its lowest point, the potential energy of the system is 0, and thus the total energy is the sum of K_{trans}, the translational kinetic energy of the driving mass:

$$E_{trans} = \frac{1}{2} M v^2 \tag{6}$$

And K_{rot}, the rotational kinetic energy of the system. This rotational kinetic energy can thus be calculated using energy conservation:

$$K_{rot} = E_{pot} - K_{trans} \tag{7}$$

The moment of inertia of the rotating system can then be calculated from the expression for rotational kinetic energy:

$$K_{rot} = \frac{I\omega^2}{2} \tag{8}$$

Where ω is the final angular velocity. Rearranging to solve for I:

$$I = \frac{2K_{rot}}{\omega^2} \tag{9}$$

Pay attention to the units. Enter your masses in kg, your lengths in m, your times in s, and your moment of inertia in kg.m². Errors are absolute errors and should be entered in the same unit as the quantity they are associated with.

Lab #2 **Rotating Dinosaurs**

7. ERROR ANALYSIS

To propagate your experimental errors, remember the simple rules we have learnt in the previous lab:

- When adding or subtracting quantities, absolute errors add up.

For example, since $K_{rot} = E_{pot} - K_{trans}$, then $dK_{rot} = dE_{pot} + dK_{trans}$

- When multiplying or dividing quantities, relative errors add up.

Example 1.

Since:

$$v = \frac{2h}{t}$$

Relative uncertainty of velocity:

$$\frac{dv}{v} = \frac{d(2)}{2} + \frac{dh}{h} + \frac{dt}{t}$$

Q. What is the absolute uncertainty of a constant value?

Ans. It's always zero.

Therefore, $d(2) = 0$

Absolute uncertainty of velocity:

$$dv = v \times \left[\frac{dh}{h} + \frac{dt}{t} \right]$$

Note: read section 8.3 to see this example with numbers.

Example 2.

Since:

$$\omega = \frac{v}{r}$$

Relative uncertainty of angular velocity:

$$\frac{d\omega}{\omega} = \frac{dv}{v} + \frac{dr}{r}$$

Absolute uncertainty of angular velocity:

$$d\omega = \omega \times \left[\frac{dv}{v} + \frac{dr}{r} \right]$$

42

3. LAB #3: THE ELECTROCARDIOGRAM

1. INTRODUCTION

1.1 Electric dipole

An electric dipole is a pair of opposite charges, +q and -q, separated by a distance d (see Fig. 1). When dealing with dipoles, we often consider something called the dipole moment, $\vec{p}$. a vector that points from -q to +q and has a magnitude of qd.

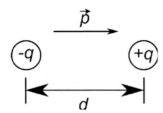

Figure 1: Schematic of an electric dipole

1.2 Muscle cells

Muscle cells have a dipole layer across the cell wall. Changes in this dipole layer trigger the contraction of muscle cells and the fibers they make up. A dipole layer is very similar to the simple electric dipole described above, the only difference being that instead of having two charges, +q and -q, you have a layer of negative and positive charges, as seen in Fig. 2. These layers of charges create a dipole moment which points across the cell wall from the inside to the outside.

In its rest state, the muscle cell is polarized, as seen in Figure 2. As stated above, the layers of charge create dipole moments pointing from the inside of the cell to the outside across the cell membrane, however since the charged layers are uniform and across a closed surface, the sum of all dipole moments is 0. As the muscle cell prepares to contract, a wave of depolarization sweeps from one side to the other of the cell, meaning that positive ions pass into the cell and cancel out the negative charge on the inside. This process is shown in Fig. 3. During this process, a dipole moment is created which points in the direction of the depolarization wave.

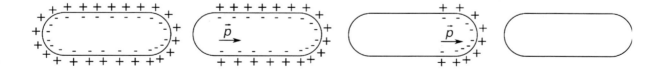

Figure 2: A muscle cell in its rest state (left) has two layers of charges with opposite sign on either side of the cell membrane, but its total dipole moment is zero. As the muscle cell depolarizes, from left to right, it acquires a dipole moment of constant magnitude, $\vec{p}$, which points in the direction of the depolarization wave.

1.3 The heart

The heart is made up of 4 main chambers: the right and left atria as well as the right and left ventricle. Blood is pumped from the atria to the ventricles and out of the heart with each beat.

As stated before, the depolarization (balancing of charge on inside and outside of cell wall) of muscle cells is what triggers heart contraction, or beating. This phenomenon allows our hearts to pump blood to our entire body at a steady pace and with great efficiency.

The entire process of the heart depolarization (beating) may be seen in Fig. 3. (a) The depolarization is triggered by the sino-auricular node (SA node), which acts much like a pacemaker, initiating the beating of the heart. (b) Once the SA node fires, the muscle cells in the heart depolarize in a wave that moves first through the atria. (c) The depolarization wave stops at the interface between the atria and the ventricles, because the tissue connecting these two regions does not transmit the electric signal. (d) However there is an atrio-ventricular node (AV node), which communicates with the atria and fires an impulse (much like the SA node) after a short time delay. (e-g) This initiates the depolarization in the ventricles.

As the depolarization wave progresses through the heart, the total dipole moment of the heart changes magnitude and direction, as can be seen in Fig. 3. The heart then repolarizes, a process not shown in the Figure.

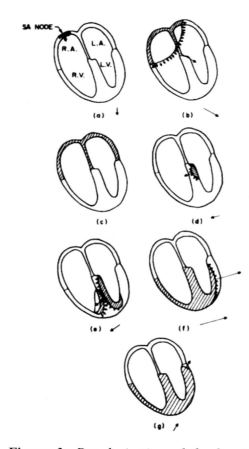

Figure 3: Depolarization of the heart. The arrows point in the direction of the dipole moment created by the sweeping of the depolarization through the heart muscle (adapted from [1]) The shaded regions are depolarized muscle cells.

1.4 The EKG

The electrocardiogram (EKG) is a common medical tool used to monitor heart activity. During an EKG, the electric potential created by the dipole moment of the heart is measured by placing electrodes at different positions on the patient's body. For a proper medical EKG, 12 different electric potential differences between electrodes placed at 7 different positions on the body are recorded simultaneously. This allows looking at the electrical signal of the heart from different angles and distances, which in turns permit an extensive characterization of the heart electrical activity. Analysis of the signal can lead to a reconstruction of the timing and direction of the depolarization and repolarization of the different compartments of the heart.

Lab #3   Electrocardiogram

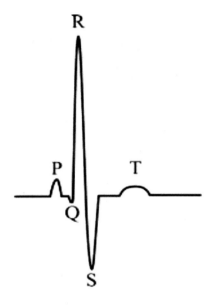

Figure 4: *Typical EKG signal and labels for the different waves. This signal represents the difference in electric potential as recorded between the left arm and the right arm.*

A typical EKG signal (measured between the left and right arm) is shown in Fig. 4. The first bump, the P-wave, is indicative of the potential created by the depolarization of the atria (Fig. 3b). Then the large spike and dip in voltage, the QRS-wave, represents the depolarization of the ventricles (Fig. 3e,f). The time gap between the P-wave and the QRS-wave, where the potential is constant, represents the delay between the completed depolarization of the atria and the firing of the AV node to trigger ventricular depolarization (Fig. 3c). Finally, the T-wave corresponds to the repolarization of the ventricle muscle cells (not represented in Fig. 3). The repolarization of the atria muscle cells is not visible in the EKG, as it is masked by the depolarization of the ventricles.

The EKG signal represented in Fig. 4 is typical of what is observed when recording the electric potential difference between the left and right arms. But note that the amplitude and the sign (positive or negative) of the electric potential will change depending on the position chosen on the surface of the body. Therefore, by changing the position of the electrodes used to monitor the EKG signal, you will obtain EKG signals with different shapes, and one can in principle fully investigate the electric potential created by the heart's electric dipole.

[1] Hobbie, R. K., The electrocardiogram as an example of electrostatics, *Am. J. Phys.* 41:824-830, 1973.

1.5 The relationship between dipole moment and potential
Approximating the heart as a dipole, we can simplify the system to look like this:

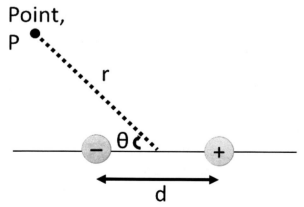

Figure 5: *Simplified version of the heart represented as a dipole; where P is some point, r distance away from the center of the dipole.*

45

Lab #3   Electrocardiogram

If the distance r is much larger than the space between the dipole, d, then the potential can be calculated using the equation:

$$V = \frac{k \cdot \rho \cdot \cos\theta}{r^2}$$

Where V is the potential, k is Coulomb's law constant, ρ is the dipole moment, θ is the angle r makes from the dipole axis, and r is the distance away from the center of the dipole.

2. Equipment

In this lab, you will have two systems at your disposal: (1) a sheet of conducting paper with pre-made dots of conductive ink, and (2) an EKG instrument.

2.1 Simulation of an electric dipole with a piece of conductive paper

The conductive paper will allow you to simulate an electric dipole and to measure the electric potential created by that dipole. The principle of the experiment is shown in the figure below.

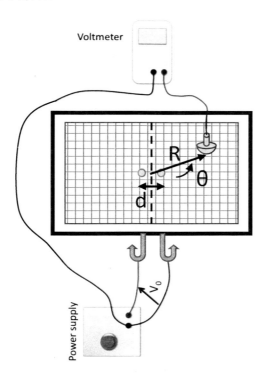

Figure 5: Schematic diagram of the experimental setup used to simulate a simple electric dipole. The two "poles" of the dipole are obtained by applying a potential difference (V_0) to two dots of conductive ink, separated by a distance *d*. You can measure the electric potential at any position on the conducting paper using a voltmeter.

As opposed to using static charges of +q and -q, it is possible to create a simulation of an electric dipole by imposing a potential difference between two points separated by a small distance on a sheet of conductive paper. Using clamps, you can secure the electrical leads of the power supply to the conductive paper. Simply clip the leads around the hooks in the bottom of the conduction paper. The hooks are connected at the back of the paper to the 2 metal dots in the center of the paper. The two dots represent the "charges" of our electric

Lab #3   **Electrocardiogram**

dipole.

The resistance of the black paper is much larger than that of the conducting dots, so compared to the "charges", the paper is effectively an insulator. However, the resistance of the voltmeter you use is even larger, making the paper appear to be a good conductor when compared to the voltmeter. Thus the paper can deliver current to the voltmeter without significantly changing the potential in the paper.

Some things to be aware of when using the black conductive paper to study the model dipole are the following:

- Because of boundary conditions, the equipotential lines (the lines of equal electric potential) always hit the edge of the paper at 90^0. Therefore, measurements made near the edge of the paper (far from the model dipole) may not directly reflect the electric potential of the dipole.

- Unlike point charges that create potentials of -infinity and +infinity where they are placed, our "charges" create finite potentials of 0V and +9V. Therefore, the electric potential close to the model dipole will not be equal to those of a real electric dipole.

- The paper is a 2D projection of the dipole, thus results may not be quantitatively equivalent to theory. Therefore you will be looking to study the qualitative rather than the quantitative nature of the dipole in this experiment.

Caution: The black conductive sheets are extremely fragile and mounted on a foam backing. To prevent damage to the sheets:

- **Never** attempt to write on the paper.

- **Avoid touching** the paper or resting your hand on it. The conductive salts on your skin can spoil the uniform resistance of the sheet.

- Measure the potential with the voltmeter using **only** the brass knob for contact.

*Note: The **voltmeter has an accuracy if 0.5%**, independent of the range.*

47

Lab #3   Electrocardiogram

2.2 Using the EKG

The EKG sensor you will use for this experiment is shown in Fig. 6. This sensor has three electrodes (also called leads) that will need to be connected to the subject's body with adhesive patches. The sensor should be already connected to a SPARK computer device that you will use to record and visualize EKG waveforms.

Figure 6: EKG sensor used for the experiment. The sensor has three leads: a ground lead (black), a negative lead (green) and a positive lead (red). Each lead needs to be attached to an adhesive patch (on the image, the red positive lead is clipped to one of these adhesive patches) stuck on the body. The EKG sensor is plugged to a SPARK computer device that allows visualizing and recording the signal.

To perform a measurement:
1) Stick one adhesive patch on the subject wrist, and clip the ground lead (black) to that patch.
2) Then chose two spots on the body between which you want to record your EKG signal, and connect the positive (green) and negative (red) lead to them using another two adhesive patches.
3) All your muscles (not just the heart) produce an electrical activity, which will be picked up by the sensor. Therefore, remain extremely still during the measurements to avoid noise due to muscle activity

Operating the SPARK
1) Press **on/off** button
2) **Plug in USB** drive to the back of the SPARK device
3) Select "**Voltage**", press "**show**".
4) Press **green arrow** to start measurement. Aim for 10 sec measurements. Press again to stop.
5) To save, press the **triangle** shape in the upper right corner and **export** your data in **ASCII format** to the USB drive.
6) Exit Voltage screen
7) Change the leads and repeat

* Warning: If you do not export in "ASCII" format your data will not open in excel, and you must do your whole measurement again.

Lab #3   **Electrocardiogram**

3. HYPOTHESIS

In this lab, we will explore the idea that the electrical activity of the heart can be approximated by that of a simple electric dipole with varying magnitude and orientation. As a lab group, you will formulate a hypothesis on how the electric potential induced by an electric dipole is qualitatively dependent on a variable of your choosing and design an experiment to test it, using both a simple experimental set-up simulating an electric dipole and an EKG instrument to measure the electric potential created by the heart.

Hint: Since we are estimating the heart as a simple dipole, the equation of focus is:

$$V = \frac{k \cdot \rho \cdot \cos\theta}{r^2}$$

Where V is the potential difference, k is Coulomb's law constant, ρ is the dipole moment, θ is the angle r makes from the dipole axis, and r is the distance away from the center of the dipole.

4. METHOD

There are two parts to this lab: 1) Conductive sheet experiment 2) EKG of the heart. Half the class will start with 1) and the other 2), then you will switch halfway through. Your TA's will instruct you which experiment to begin with at the start of lab.

4.1 Conductive sheet experiment (groups of 2)

In order to refresh your memory about the electrical potential created by a dipole you will first study the equipotential lines of a simple fixed dipole using the provided conducting paper.

- On your black conducting paper sheet, record the location of the two silver dots of conducting paint in the center separated by d = 1 cm.

- Attach the electrical leads from the power supply to the hooks at the bottom of the paper. A schematic of the setup is seen in Figure 6.

- Now adjust the knob of the power supply so that it is outputting a potential difference of 8V. You can check what that the difference in electric potential provided by the power supply is by attaching the voltmeter leads to the power supply terminals.

- Check that when you place the lead in contact with the pin connected to the 8V terminal of the power supply (red) you measure a potential of 8V. As well, ensure that the potentials that you are measuring on the paper are in the range of a couple volts, not millivolts.

49

Lab #3   **Electrocardiogram**

Measurements:

- Start with the vertical line down the center of the dipole. This should have the same voltage, so you can get an estimate for the uncertainty in your voltage reading. Record 10 points along this line, and use the greatest distance from the average voltage as your uncertainty.

- Use the uncertainty of the voltage to group points together. (ex. The 4.0 V ± 0.2 V equipotential line includes all points whose voltage is between 3.8 V and 4.2 V.) You should have a voltage range in mind when recording points. If you are working on the 4.0 V ± 0.2 V equipotential line, you should search on the paper for 10 points with this voltage, and record their positions. Then move on to the next V range.

- You need to have **7 equipotential lines**, with ~10 points on each (that's 1 down the middle, and 3 on each side).

- Make a schematic drawing of the equipotential lines created at the dipole, indicating the value of the potential on each line you draw. **When you are done, also draw the electric field lines of the dipole.**

- The collection of data should take ~60 min. Check with your TA that you have observed the correct overall shape of the electric potential field before moving on to the next step.

4.2 EKG (groups of 4)

Take 5 minutes to discuss with your group and decide on a hypothesis you would like to test related to the heart's dipole moment. Remember, the equation of focus is equation (1), which has 2 options of variables which you can change:

    I.   The distance from the dipole, r.

    II.   The angle from the dipole, θ.

Whichever one you choose, remember all parameters in this equation must stay the same, except for the 1 parameter you choose to change; either I) or II).

When graphing your results, we are looking for a <u>linear</u> relationship, which means you will either be plotting:

    I.   Varying the distance from the dipole, r.

$$V \text{ vs. } \frac{1}{r^2}$$

$$slope = k \cdot \rho \cdot cos\theta \qquad \text{y-int} = 0$$

$$\text{Experimental dipole moment: } \rho = \frac{slope}{k \cdot cos\theta}$$

Lab #3   **Electrocardiogram**

II.   Varying the angle from the dipole, θ.

$$V \text{ vs. } \cos\theta$$

$$slope = \frac{k \cdot \rho}{r^2} \qquad\qquad \text{y-int} = 0$$

$$\text{Experimental dipole moment: } \rho = \frac{slope \cdot r^2}{k}$$

*Note: Your experimental dipole moment **absolutely must** have an uncertainty.*

With your slope, you can calculate your answer for the dipole moment of the heart by rearranging the slope equation above. Use this value to compare with theory to confirm or reject your hypothesis. This time you were not given the experimental dipole moment of the human heart that you need to confirm or reject your hypothesis. You must research this for yourself, and make sure you include this value in your introduction, with the source. Do not be discouraged if your results do not agree with theory or what you expected. It is important to explain the problems with the model and significant sources of error in the discussion. Absolutely <u>do not</u> try to force your results to fit a specific answer.

Note: Remember, you must be able to relate this experiment back to the conductive paper experiment in your report. Think about qualitative ways they are connected.

5. REPORT INFORMATION

<u>**In pairs**</u>, write a short report (you should aim for 4 pages of text maximum, plus title page, figures, tables and references).

Research the Dipole moment of the heart in papers to get a comparison to your experimental value. Papers are accessible on McMaster Campus through the libraries and MacSecure.

Refer to Part I: Chapter 10 of the lab manual to learn how to analyze the data you have collected, and write a good report.

Return your completed report to the 1AA3 drop boxes outside BSB B110, or as per your TA's instruction. Check Avenue announcements.

[handwritten margin note, left side: 1.466, 1.481, 1.50, 1.437, 1.486, 1.466, 1.50]

[handwritten notes:]
- method
- figures
- sample calcs
- graphs
- tables

- sources in intro
  ↳ heart's dipole moment (# + source)

Lab #4   Magnetotactic Bacteria

4. LAB #4: MAGNETOTACTIC BACTERIA

1. INTRODUCTION

1.1 Magnetotactic bacteria

The Earth's magnetic field, also known as the geomagnetic field, plays a role in the orientation and movement of a wide variety of organisms, and magnetotactic bacteria (MTB) are a typical example of such organisms. MTB are a heterogeneous group of prokaryote microorganisms with a variety of morphologies, which include spherical-shaped (cocci), rod-shaped (bacilli), curved (vibrio), and helical (spirillum). They have a wide ecological distribution, from freshwater to marine ecosystems. In some environments, MTB have been shown to be the dominant species of the bacterial population, which suggests they have an important ecological role.

Magnetotactic bacteria contain a distinctive organelle called the magnetosome, which is made of a chain of magnetic particles enclosed in a lipid membrane. These particles, usually 35 to 120 nm in size, are made either of magnetite (Fe_3O_4) or greigite (Fe_3S_4). In the magnetosome their magnetic moments are aligned, such that they provide a permanent magnetic dipole moment to the bacterium. Since the axis of the magnetosome is roughly aligned with the axis of the bacterium, this magnetic moment is also aligned with the axis of the bacterium.

Because of their magnetic dipole moment, when MTB are placed in a magnetic field, they experience a torque if their axis is positioned at an angle relative to the direction of the magnetic field. This ultimately causes the bacteria to align with the magnetic field, just as a compass needle would. As a consequence, MTB tends to swim along geomagnetic field lines. MTB are microaerophillic organisms, meaning that they are only able to survive in environments with low oxygen concentrations. It is believed that they use the geomagnetic field to move to microaerophillic environments, generally found in the lower layers of lakes and oceans. In support of this theory, MTB found in the Northern Hemisphere generally swim in the direction of the magnetic field, which in this part of the world points downward, while MTB in the Southern Hemisphere, generally swim in the direction opposite to that of the magnetic field, which in that part of the world points upwards. While most MTB strains are polar, meaning that they swim in one direction in the presence of a magnetic field (either in the direction of the magnetic field or in the direction opposite to that of the magnetic field), some (including the *Magnetospirilum Magneticum* strain AMB-1 that you will study in this lab) are axial, meaning that they can reverse their polarity (i.e. each bacterium can move in the direction of the magnetic field or opposite to the magnetic field).

MTB are of interest to scientists and engineers for many different reasons. MTB have been shown to remove heavy metals and radionuclides from wastewater and are being investigated as possible water purifying agents. The iron particles they synthesize are more uniform and of better quality than those that can be produced industrially at the moment, therefore there is great interest in using them as chemical reactors for the production of magnetic particles. Commercial uses of bacterial magnetite particles have been suggested, which includes the manufacture of magnetic tapes and printing inks, magnetic targeting of

Lab #4   **Magnetotactic Bacteria**

pharmaceuticals, cell separation, and contrast enhancement in magnetic resonance imaging. Ultrafine-grained magnetite particles found on a Martian meteorite and resembling magnetsome crystals have been cited as putative evidence for ancient extraterrestrial life.

1.2 MTB motion

MTB tend to align with magnetic fields, however they are not pulled by them. Instead, MTBs propel themselves by rotating their flagella. One can usually assume that flagella provide a force of constant magnitude, F_P, which propels the bacterium forward. Opposing that force is a viscous force, f, such that in steady state: $|F_P| = |f|$. For a small object such as a bacterium moving through in an aqueous medium, the viscous force should be related to the object speed, v, according to:

$$|f| = 6\pi\eta R v \tag{1}$$

Where η is the viscosity of the surrounding fluid and R is the so-called Stokes radius of the object. For a spherical object, R would simply be the radius of the object. But for an elongated object like a bacterium moving parallel to its long axis, there is a more complicated relationship.

1.3 MTB orientation in a magnetic field

The tendency that MTBs have to align with the local magnetic field can be countered by Brownian motion, which is the collisions between MTBs and the molecules in the surrounding medium. In order to determine whether the effect of the magnetic field will dominate over the effect of Brownian motion, one can compare the decrease in potential energy, U, which a bacterium with dipole moment μ achieves by aligning its dipole moment with a magnetic field of strength B:

$$U = \mu B$$

With the kinetic energy imparted to the bacterium by Brownian motion:

$$K = kT$$

Where **k is the Boltzmann constant**, and T is the temperature in Kelvin. If $U \gg K$, then the effect of the magnetic field is strong enough for the bacterium to align with the magnetic field, whereas if $U \ll K$, then Brownian motion prevents the bacterium to align with the magnetic field. In general, the magnetic dipole moment of MTB is found to be just large enough for the magnetic interaction with the geomagnetic field (which is about 50 µT) to dominate over Brownian motion at room temperature.

One can quantify how aligned the bacteria are with the magnetic field by considering the angle α between the direction of the magnetic field and the axis of the bacteria. If $\alpha=0$, the bacterium is aligned with the field. One can show that for a population of MTB with dipole moment μ placed in a magnetic field of strength B, the distribution of angles (or the probability of finding a certain angle, α) of the bacteria is characterized by:

$$P = A \cdot e^{\frac{\mu B}{kT} \cos\alpha}$$

53

Lab #4   Magnetotactic Bacteria

The width of this distribution, defined here as $\alpha_{1/2}$ and measured from half the full height of the distribution, is characterized by:

$$\cos\left(\alpha_{\frac{1}{2}}\right) = 1 - \ln(2) \cdot \frac{kT}{\mu B} \tag{2}$$

With this equation above, we can calculate the dipole moment, as long as you know the temperature, T, (room temperature ~293 K) and the magnetic field, B.

2. EQUIPMENT

In this lab, you will not be asked to record your own experimental data, instead you will use pre-recorded movies of MTB exposed to different viscosity and magnetic field conditions. The link to this database of movies will be given to you on the course website.

To analyze bacterial trajectories, you will use a free software called ImageJ, and a plugin written for this software called MTrackJ.

2.1 Bacterial Motion Measurement tutorial

This tutorial, which was written by Rohan Nadkarni, will walk you through the procedure for 1) downloading the three programs needed to carry out this lab (ImageJ, MTrackJ and VirtualDub), 2) opening the videos you will be working on using ImageJ, 3) calibrating the size of the videos by entering the correct unit in IMageJ, 4) using the straight line measurement tool in ImageJ and 5) using MTrackJ.

1) Program Info and Downloading Instructions

For ImageJ

ImageJ is a program that allows users to manipulate images/videos in various ways. Similar to Adobe Photoshop, this program can be used to adjust the colour, contrast, texture, style, and other properties of an image/video. This program can also be used to analyze and take measurements.

Download ImageJ from the following link: http://rsbweb.nih.gov/ij/download.html

Although ImageJ has a wide variety of functions that you may utilize in upper years for other courses (not just Physics), for the purpose of this lab we will only be using it for particle analysis. We will need to download a plugin that serves that particular function.

Lab #4   Magnetotactic Bacteria

For MTrackJ

MTrackJ is an ImageJ plugin that allows users to analyze the motion of particles and measure properties such as position, distance, velocity, etc.

Download MTrackJ from the following link: http://www.imagescience.org/meijering/software/mtrackj/ (Note: You need to download **2 files** from this link and move them to the Plugins folder of ImageJ; only then will the plugin work).

For VirtualDub

ImageJ is only able to open uncompressed AVI files. The videos that we capture in the lab are compressed. VirtualDub is a program that allows us to save any AVI file in its uncompressed form.

Download VirtualDub from the following link: http://virtualdub.sourceforge.net/ Also download the Combined Community Codel Pack (CCCP) from the following link: http://www.cccp-project.net/ and save it to your desktop or anywhere else on your computer. Only then will VirtualDub work.

2) Opening a Video

The easiest is to download the uncompressed video. If you can do that, you do not need VirtualDub and you can go directly to step 2. If you cannot download the uncompressed video, then download the smaller compressed video. You then have have to uncompress the video using VirtualDub (step 1) before you can open it with ImageJ (step 2). and then set preferences. Follow these steps to successfully open a video:

Step 1

Open VirtualDub. Select **File -> Open video file**. Choose the desired video. After the video opens, select **File -> Save as AVI**.

The video will now be saved as an uncompressed AVI file.

Step 2

Open ImageJ. The menu panel will open, which looks like this:

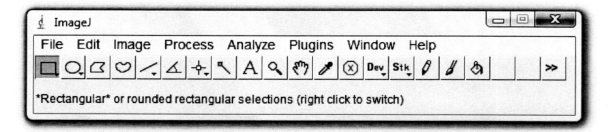

Lab #4 — Magnetotactic Bacteria

It may look different depending on your operating system.

Select **File -> Open**. Choose the video file that you uncompressed using VirtualDub (if you do not open an uncompressed AVI file, an error message will appear saying "Unsupported Compression").

After you open the desired file, the following window pops up:

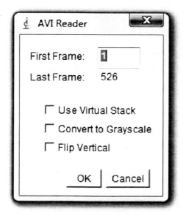

This will allow us to open either the whole movie or a small portion within. The last frame will be set at whatever the length of your movie is. In this case, the movie I am opening is 526 frames long. I would recommend that you open only a small portion of the movie at a time (e.g. First Frame = 1, Last Frame = 100), because if you try to open the full movie (which might be 300+ frames long), it will take more time to open it and you may experience lag. So I suggest that you open frames 1 to 100 first, analyze the portion of the movie (we'll get to that later), then open frames 100-200, analyze, then open frames 200-300, and so on (you may not need to analyze the full movie anyway, because the bacteria of interest may only be present in one specific interval of your movie, and so you can open the corresponding number of frames).

Leave the three boxes at the bottom unchecked, and **click OK**. The video will then load and open (loading time depends on the number of frames opened).

3) Calibration of Units

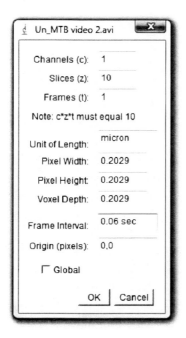

We need to calibrate the units of length and time for ImageJ, which is vital for measurements. We need to set these units. Select **Image -> Properties**. The following window will pop up. Make the following changes (except the number of slices (z); keep that at whatever value it appears to be for you):

Step 1 - Length

The default unit of length for ImageJ is the pixel. We will be using micrometers (or microns). We first need to know how many microns are in one pixel. The ratio has been calculated for you: there are approximately 4.9286 pixels in 1 micron, so there are approximately 0.2029 microns in 1 pixel. **The pixel width, pixel height, and voxel depth should all be changed to the same value, which is 0.2029 (for ALL students).**

Lab #4   Magnetotactic Bacteria

Step 2 - Time

The frame interval is the amount of time that passes between each adjacent frame as the movie plays. It depends on the frame rate of the movie and the camera settings that were adjusted while filming the movie. **The frame interval is located at the top left hand corner of the movie window in brackets. Find it and type it in the box.** In my example, it is 0.06 sec. Unlike the units (which are the same for everyone), the frame interval will most likely vary among students.

Note - Do NOT change the number of slices (z). In my example, it is 10. Do not change yours. Keep it at whatever value it appears to be for you. It is just equal to the number of frames of the opened video, which will vary among students. If you accidentally did change it and forgot what the original value was, just close the video, reopen it, and make the other changes for units and frame interval as described above.

For the purposes of this lab, whenever you open a video file on ImageJ, you must remember to change the image properties as listed above.

Click Ok. The resolution of the image (129.86 x103.88 microns = 640x512 pixels) should be displayed at the top.

4) Straight Line Measurement Tool

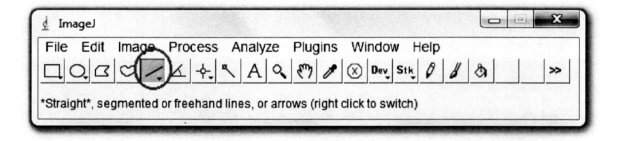

The straight line tool allows for the measurement of the distance between two points on an image/video. Once you draw a line and then click somewhere else, the line will disappear, hence it is only used for measurement and is not a drawing tool. When drawing a line, its length (in microns) is shown in the ImageJ panel. For example (after zooming in onto a particular bacterium):

Lab #4   Magnetotactic Bacteria

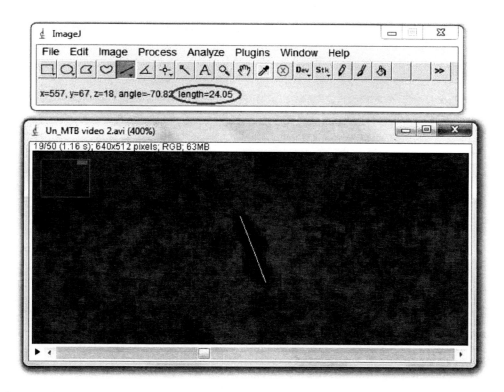

5) Using MTrackJ

On your ImageJ menu panel, select **Plugins -> MTrackJ**.

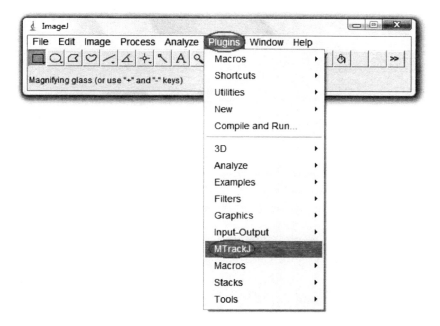

This will open the MTrackJ menu panel, which provides us with various options for particle tracking.

Lab #4   Magnetotactic Bacteria

The panel is shown on the next page:

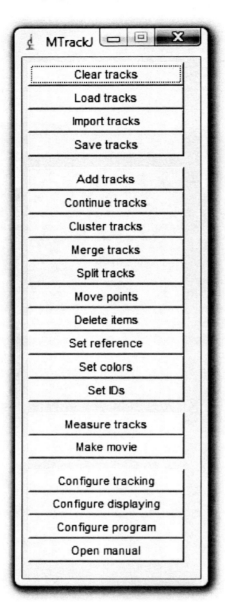

The following are simple descriptions of the modes on this panel (they are not in the order that they are listed on the panel):

Add tracks – This mode will let you create a track for a bacterium of interest. At a particular frame at which the bacterium is visible on the movie, put the mouse pointer on the front end (edge) of the bacterium and click on it. MTrackJ will automatically move to the next frame once you do this, where the bacterium has moved by a few microns. Click on the front end of the bacterium now and again you will automatically be moved to the next frame. Repeat this process until you

Lab #4 — Magnetotactic Bacteria

generate a long enough bacterial path. Here is an example of a path (from one point to the other with n number of frames in between):

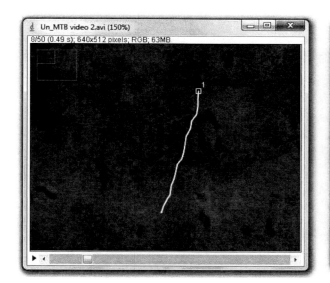 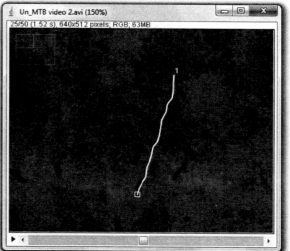

Continue Tracks – This function allows you to edit a track (or path) that has already been constructed. Simply click on a track to select and edit it in any frame.

Delete Tracks – Choose this function and then click on a particular track to delete it.

Configure Displaying – Choosing this function opens up another panel that allows you to play with physical properties of the track, such as its style and colour.

Make Movie – You can construct tracks for various bacteria and then choose this button to make a movie, where all tracks are visible.

Measure Tracks – Make sure that you have altered the Image Properties discussed on page 3 before you use this function. Selecting it provides you with measurements such as position and velocity (with their standard deviations) of bacterial paths.

Lab #4   **Magnetotactic Bacteria**

3. Hypothesis

In this lab, we will investigate the behavior of magnetotactic bacteria in the presence of a magnetic field. You will formulate a hypothesis related to the speed or orientation of the movement of magnetotactic bacteria, and you will test your hypothesis as by tracking the motion of many such bacteria as seen in movies recorded in different conditions.

There are 2 main equations, and many hypothesis options to choose from, so choose whichever one interests you more. Whatever hypothesis you choose, remember you must be able to confirm or reject your hypothesis from your experimental results.

3.1 MTB motion

For this topic, the main equation you are using is:

$$|f| = 6\pi\eta R v$$

There are many experiments that can be conducted around this equation. A couple sample questions you can ask for this lab are:

- How would you expect the speed of a bacterium, v, to depend on its length, L?
- How does the velocity change when you increase magnetic field or viscosity?

Note: These are just some examples. If there is another idea you have, talk to your TA to see if it is possible.

3.2 MTB orientation

For this topic, the main equation you are using is:

$$\cos\left(\alpha_{\frac{1}{2}}\right) = 1 - \ln(2) \cdot \frac{kT}{\mu B}$$

A couple sample questions you can ask for this lab are:

- How does the dipole moment compare to the expected dipole moment in literature?
- How does the most probable angle change with varying magnetic field or viscosity?

Note: These are just some examples. If there is another idea you have, talk to your TA to see if it is possible.

4. Method

You will not be preforming the experiment in the typical fashion as you have all term. The whole experiment can be done from home if you wish. There will be a help center open during a normal lab time if you wish to sit in the classroom to meet a group and start working, but it is not required that you show up to the lab for this experiment. Check the avenue

Lab #4   Magnetotactic Bacteria

announcements for the schedule. The analysis should be done as a group, which means that you could either meet to work together, or that you could each do some data analysis and then pool your data together. When you are done, upload the results of your analysis (in one or more Excel spreadsheets) in the "**Lab #4 dropbox**" on Avenue.

4.1 MTB motion

In groups of 4:

Take time to discuss amongst your group to decide on an experiment. If you are unsure of what to do, check out the hypothesis section above. All graphical relationships are linear in this course unless otherwise specified.

There are a couple parameters which you can vary. Remember when given an equation with many parameters, you can only vary one parameter to test its effect. Whichever experiment you decide on, remember your slope and y-intercept must have an uncertainty.

    I.   Changing Viscosity, n

Example 1. If you are testing the relationship between velocity and viscosity:

$$\frac{1}{v} = \left[\frac{6\pi}{|f|} * R\right] \cdot n$$

You must plot: $\frac{1}{v}$ vs. n

Using many videos of different solution concentration, through Imagej you will need to measure the velocity and estimate the R value. The R value is a dimensionless quantity, which quantifies how spherical an object is. Ellipticity is a similar dimensionless quantity that you can estimate R with. What shape do you think is appropriate for these bacteria?

The final result is the force found through the slope and an expected y-intercept of 0:

    The slope is: $\frac{6\pi}{|f|}R$ **The y-int is:** 0

Note: This means you must choose bacteria with all the same size, within uncertainty.

Your final result will be to find the force from your slope.

$$|f| = \frac{6\pi}{Slope} R$$

Example 2. If you are testing the relationship between force and viscosity:

$$|f| = 6\pi R v * (n)$$

You must plot: $|f|$ vs n

Lab #4   **Magnetotactic Bacteria**

Using many videos of different solution concentration, through Imagej you will need to measure the acceleration, the average velocity.

You will need to estimate the mass of a bacteria for the force (F=ma). Bacteria are mostly water, which you can find the density of. You can also measure the volume. This will give you the mass.

The final result is the force found through the slope and an expected y-intercept of 0:

$$\textbf{The slope is}: 6\pi vR \qquad\qquad \textbf{The y-int is}: 0$$

Note: This means all your bacteria must have the same <u>*average velocity within error*</u> *and size.*

This means your final result is the radius of your bacteria. How does this value compare to the length and width of your chosen bacteria?

II.   Length

Length appears in equation (1) as: $\ln(\frac{L}{D})$. Therefore, when graphing your linear relationship, you will want $\ln(\frac{L}{D})$ on your x-axis.

Example 1. If you are testing the relationship between force and length:

The radius you must use is the Stoke's radius:

$$R = a + b\ln\left(L/D\right)$$

Where L is the length of the bacteria and D its diameter, while a and b are constant parameters to be determined. Subbing this in to equation 1:

$$1/v = (6\pi n/|f|) * (a + b * \ln\left(\frac{L}{D}\right))$$

$$1/v = (6\pi nb/|f|)* \ln\left(\frac{L}{D}\right) + 6\pi na/|f|$$

$$\text{You must plot: } 1/v \text{ vs } \ln(\tfrac{L}{D})$$

Using 1 video, and many different bacteria, through Imagej you will need to measure the acceleration, the average velocity, the L and D.

You will need to estimate the mass of a bacteria for the force (F=ma). Bacteria are mostly water, which you can find the density of. You can also measure the volume. This will give you the mass.

63

Lab #4   **Magnetotactic Bacteria**

The final result is the parameters *a* and *b* through the slope and y-intercept:

The slope is: $6\pi nb/|f|$ **The y-int is**: $6\pi na/|f|$

* You can make an estimate of R to remove the a and b parameters as well using this hypothesis for the force alone as a final result. *The R value is a dimensionless quantity, which quantifies how spherical an object is. Ellipticity is a similar dimensionless quantity that you can estimate R with. What shape do you think is appropriate for these bacteria?*

III.   Magnetic field

If you vary the magnetic field in relation to test the relationship to the velocity, you must plot: v vs. B. This means you must have bacteria of all the same length and diameter, and in the same viscosity.

Since you do not have a direct mathematical relationship to test for this experiment, you must think about how you are going to formulate a hypothesis.

- What do you expect to happen (using specific reasons from literature).

Note: It is always a good idea to check with your TA to make sure you are on the right track with your experiment. Check the course website to see when your TA's are answering questions on the forums.

Data Requirements (Motion)

Length vs **force or speed**
Your goal for this lab is to crudely investigate how the speed, force or viscosity of magnetotactic bacteria varies with their length. For this, you will need to download one of the movies (see content section), open it using ImageJ, and to track at least nine different bacteria using MTrackJ (at least 20 frames/track). Then use Excel to plot f, v, or n as a function of R (the bacterium size, which you can measure using ImageJ).
(*** Groups of 4 will have to do at least 12 bacteria)

Viscocity vs **Bacteria speed or force**
Your goal for this lab is to crudely investigate how the force or speed of magnetotactic bacteria varies with the glycerol content of the solution in which the bacteria are swimming, or force. For this, you will need to download at least three the movies, open them using ImageJ, and to track at least three different bacteria from each movie using MTrackJ (at least 20 frames/track). You then need to use the link on avenue to find viscosity from g (the % amount of glycerol in the solution). Then use Excel to plot f or v (the average speed of a bacterium) as a function of viscosity.
(*** groups of 4 will have to do at least 4 videos, with 3 bacteria each)

Lab #4 Magnetotactic Bacteria

4.2 MTB orientation

In groups of 4:

Take 15 mins to decide on an experiment. If you are unsure of what to do, check out the hypothesis section above. This experiment is the only non-linear graph you will be making in this course.

Using a sample size of 50 bacteria, the probability curve of MTB for a specific magnetic field and viscosity will look like the figure below. To gather this data you measure the angle of the 50 bacteria. Some of the angles will be more popular, since the bacteria in a higher magnetic field want to go the direction of the magnetic field lines. A histogram shows the popularity of certain angles, with the peak of the curve being the most popular angle.

Histograms use bins, which is like slicing a cake. With a bin size of 5, any angles between 0°-5° are in the same slice, and 5°-10° are the next slice. The probability shows how big each slice is.

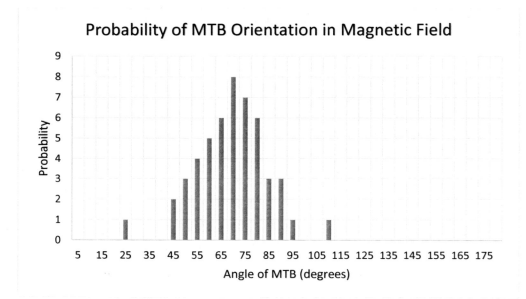

Histogram in Excel [1]

In order to create the above graph, you must have the "Analysis Toolpak" installed in excel. To install, follow the directions below.

- A. On the **File** menu, click **Options**.
- B. Click **Add-Ins** in the navigation pane.
- C. In the **Manage** list, select **Excel Add-ins**, and then click **Go**.
- D. In the **Add-Ins** dialog box, make sure that the **Analysis ToolPak** check box under **Add-Ins available** is selected, and then click **OK**.

To create a Histogram:

Lab #4　　　　　　　　　　　　　　　　　　　　Magnetotactic Bacteria

A. On the **Data** tab, click **Data Analysis** in the **Analysis** group.

B. In the **Data Analysis** dialog box, click **Histogram**, and then click **OK**.

C. In the **Input Range** box, insert your angle data.

D. In the **bin range**, insert a list of bins. There is an excel template on the course website with a list from 0° to 180°, with width of 5°. Try bin sizes from 2°-6° and look for the smoothest distribution of data.

E. Under **Output Options**, click **New Workbook**, select the **Chart Output** check box, and then click **OK**.

F. You now have a new table, with bin and frequency. Use a **column graph**, with **bin on the x-axis** and **frequency on the y-axis**.

[1] https://support.microsoft.com/en-us/kb/214269

I. Finding the dipole moment of the bacteria

By measuring a large number of bacteria (at least 100) at a specific magnetic field and viscosity, you can get an even more refined image than the graph above. With this, you can accurately read the $\alpha_{1/2}$ value.

To get the $\alpha_{1/2}$ value

- After you have plotted your histogram, add the **moving average trend line**. Now you can more clearly see where the peak in your data is located.

- Find the width of your data at half the maximum height:

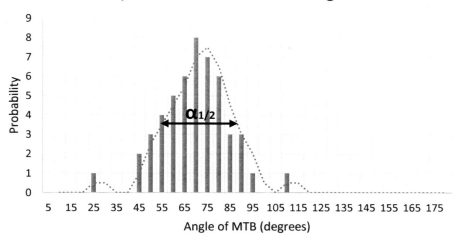

Lab #4   **Magnetotactic Bacteria**

Where:

$$\alpha_{1/2} = 90°\text{-}55° = 35° \pm 5°;\ \textit{Note: uncertainty comes from the bin size.}$$

- Now that you have $\alpha_{1/2}$, the value can be inserted into the following rearranged equation, to solve for the dipole moment, μ.

$$\cos\left(\alpha_{\frac{1}{2}}\right) = 1 - \ln(2) \cdot \frac{kT}{\mu B}$$

- Don't forget, you must compare this value to one found in literature.

Remember: The more data you collect, the more accurate and easy to analyze your data will become. We've given minimum values to reach, but it is a good idea to gather more data than the mentioned values above.

II.   Varying Magnetic field

  Using a smaller sample size of approximately 33 bacteria, you can test how magnetic field changes the preferred orientation of the bacteria between 3 different magnetic fields.

- What do you expect to happen (using specific reasons from literature).

- How can you quantify the change of preferred angle? How are you going to display your result?

Remember: The more data you collect, the more accurate, and easy to analyze your data will become. We've given minimum values to reach, but it is a good idea to gather more data than the mentioned values above.

Data Requirements (orientation)

Bacteria direction in a magnetic field (group of 4)
Your goal for this lab is to crudely investigate how well the direction of motion of the magnetotactic bacteria aligns with the applied magnetic field, by looking at the dipole moment. Choose 1 video with a medium magnetic field strength (12-28 G). Use a sample size of 50 bacteria, and track each of them for ~5-7 steps (enough that you can tell the direction they are going). Calculate the angle from the horizontal for all bacteria. Use lab analysis on pg 65 to find the dipole moment and compare with theory (type in google "dipole moment of magnetotactic bacteria" and find a source; the dipole moment density must be converted to dipole moment using the volume of a human heart).

67

Lab #4   **Magnetotactic Bacteria**

Bacteria Direction vs. **magnetic field strength**

Your goal for this lab is to crudely investigate how the direction of motion of the magnetotactic bacteria varies with the strength of the applied magnetic field. For this, you will need to download four of the movies on avenue, open them using ImageJ, and to track three different bacteria from each movie using MTrackJ (at least 20 steps/track). Then use Excel to plot the average angle of travel as a function B (the applied magnetic field). Must do research to compare theory to experiment.

(***for groups of 3, use 3 videos)

5. REPORT INFORMATION

 In your group, write a report (you should aim for 5 pages of text maximum, plus title page, figures and references).

Groups of 3-4 students are expected. **Groups of less than 3 students must complete the work of a 3 person group. No groups over 4 people will be accepted.**

Return your completed report to the drop boxes outside BSB B110, as per your TA's instruction.

This course pack is made in accordance with the University's Fair Dealing Policy for sale to and use by students enrolled in the course of study for which it was made. This course pack may also include copyright-protected material pursuant to permissions granted by the copyright holder. Any reproduction or other use of this material is strictly forbidden.

COURSEWARE IS NON-RETURNABLE

PHYSICS 1AA3
385412

McMaster University

Custom Publishing
Everything in one book.

The Campus Store and Media Production Services are proud partners in the production of this custom publication. All material is printed with copyright permission.

This custom publication is non-returnable

9 780666 385413